5-INGREDIENT VEGAN COOKING

60 Approachable Plant-Based Recipes with a Few Ingredients and *Lots of Flavor*

KATE FRIEDMAN

Creator of
Herbivore's Kitchen

PAGE STREET
PUBLISHING CO.

PAGE STREET
PUBLISHING CO.

First published in 2021 by

Page Street Publishing Co.

27 Congress Street, Suite 105

Salem, MA 01970

www.pagestreetpublishing.com

Distributed by Macmillan, sales in Canada by The Canadian Manda Group.

25   24   23   22   21   1   2   3   4   5

ISBN-13: 978-1-64567-273-9

ISBN-10: 1-64567-273-5

Library of Congress Control Number: 2020948809

Cover and book design by Kylie Alexander and Meg Baskis for Page Street Publishing Co. Photography by Kate Friedman

Printed and bound in China

DEDICATION

To the 7th Street Gang. Thank you to Levi (10), Ellie (8), Avery (10), Eden (7), Ike (8) and Cy (7) for telling me that my kitchen always smells good; being diplomatic when my recipes are "not the best, but not the worst either"; stopping in the middle of a game of tag to try something new; being my hand models when asked; and rewarding me with an enthusiastic thumbs-up when I finally get it right.

Contents

Introduction

Welcome! I'm so grateful to you for inviting me into your homes to share a meal with you. A lot of time, effort and consideration went into every part of this book, so the fact that you've decided to add it to your collection means so much. My heart is full.

A lot of vegan cookbooks dedicate their introductions to the benefits of a vegan diet—from personal health gains, to environmental sustainability, to just being a kinder human to the creatures with whom we share the planet. Without question, these topics are incredibly worthwhile. They are the arguments that persuaded me to change my own diet. If digging into these subjects is of interest to you, you can find a list of great books and articles on my blog, Herbivore's Kitchen, to learn more. I update it frequently. If you're just here for the food, I won't hold you up by pleading my case on these topics. However, if you will indulge me for just a few short paragraphs, I do want to use this introduction to talk about something else that I think hinders the shift to a healthier, more sustainable, kinder diet—and that is the concept of perfection.

Have you ever tried a diet and failed? Yeah, me too. Plenty of times. At least by my old definition of failed. In my mind, the word "failed" meant "not executed with perfection." A lofty (and highly unattainable) goal for sure. Maybe it's a product of age or maybe it just took me longer to catch on (likely the latter), but I don't think about failure that way anymore. Instead, I have a favorite quote that I like to remind myself of: "Don't make perfect the enemy of the good."

If you subscribe to the argument (and I do) that eating a plant-based diet will lead to a healthier you, living on a healthier planet, then it stands to reason that eating this way some of the time will reap the same proportional benefits. Many vegans have a tendency to frame the decision to avoid animal-based products as an all-or-nothing proposition, making it incredibly intimidating to newcomers. Actually, it makes it incredibly intimidating to me as well. Here's the truth: I am not the perfect vegan. I love vegan cooking. I love the way I feel when I eat vegan. I especially love the earth-saving heart swell that comes on when the conveyor belt at the grocery store is loaded with vegetables and grains. Look at me! Saving the planet one ingredient at a time!

Sometimes though, with family and work and travel, my execution isn't flawless. I do my best. Sometimes my best is ordering a vegetarian dish when I'm out or heating up ready-made sauces (my favorite being Maya Kaimal) because that's what I have the energy for. I'm telling you this because I want to be clear that I don't have it all dialed in all the time. And I didn't write this book because I expect you to either. In the end, I just want the club to be bigger. Whatever you call yourself—vegan veteran, vegan lite or vegan curious—you're welcome in my tribe, and I think you'll find that the recipes in this book make it easier (and tastier) to eat vegan than you might have imagined.

Kate Friedman

The 5-Ingredient Approach

When I first approached vegan cooking, I found the list of potential ingredients daunting. I shunned tofu. I'd never cooked with jackfruit or tempeh, let alone heard of aquafaba or rejuvelac (and by the way, if you've never heard of aquafaba or rejuvelac either, you're in the right place). It took a while, but eventually I hit my rhythm. I learned how to cook with a variety of new and different ingredients—like miso paste, nutritional yeast and curry powder. Pretty soon I was hooked—hooked on the idea of making vegan food taste good. Really, really good.

To do this though, I used a long list of vegan-friendly ingredients. "The more, the merrier!" I'd say. "Fill your fridge!" and "Pack your pantry!" I'd sing. If you follow my blog, you know this about me. I like creating vegan recipes with a lengthy list of ingredients. And, I think, to a great outcome. You can make some really incredible vegan dishes with a wide variety of ingredients. Things like [insert shameless blog plug]: Veggie Loaded Vegan Pho, No Coq au Vin and Vegan Moo Shu Pizza. Incredible enough to sway even the most dedicated of omnivores.

It would follow then, that stepping outside of my comfort zone and writing a cookbook embracing the 5-ingredient concept was a bit new to me. I quickly learned, though, that really good vegan food doesn't have to be complicated. You can make tasty, healthy meals with few ingredients. Now I'm a convert. Well, at least some of the time. I've just come to love having easy recipes that can often be made with what I have on hand.

Building this list of ingredients was no easy task. I spent a lot of time browsing other 5-, 7- and 10-ingredient cookbooks. I evaluated how other authors approached the concept and read the reviews. What did readers like? What turned them off? In the end, these were my two takeaways from home chefs: (1) I can forgive you a very small list of staple ingredients that won't count toward the five ingredients. After all, if three of the five ingredients are olive oil, salt and pepper, this would be a very boring cookbook indeed; and (2) Please don't ask me to open a jar of commercially produced spaghetti sauce and add it to pasta. I don't need a cookbook to tell me that.

"Fair enough," I decided. And these two takeaways became the principles that guided each and every recipe in this cookbook.

PRINCIPLE #1: A SMALL LIST OF VEGAN STAPLES. TEN, TO BE EXACT.

This principle—creating a very small list of staple ingredients—was a challenge for me. I swapped "this" for "that" and then swapped it back. I waffled. Could I extend it to fifteen? Twenty? In the end, though, it was incredibly important to me that I do everything I could to honor the 5-ingredient concept. What I eventually realized was that there really is a small subset of ingredients that I use over and over again. Ingredients that, without their inclusion, would leave my recipes lacking. Before long, this list wrote itself. So here it is—the list of my vegan staples:

Oils: Extra-Virgin Olive Oil, Coconut Oil, Safflower Oil

Vinegars/Sauces: Tamari Sauce, Rice Wine Vinegar

Fruits/Vegetables: Onions, Garlic, Lemons (fresh lemon juice & zest)

Spices: Salt, Pepper

Ten ingredients in all. I know this list varies from what you might find on a pantry staples list in many non-vegan cookbooks. For example, I picked three different types of cooking oils and included both lemons and tamari sauce on my list. I decided to forego apple cider and red wine vinegar and instead chose rice wine vinegar. This is because I use these ingredients more commonly and I think that they play really well in vegan cooking. Most of these ingredients you likely have in your kitchen already.

PRINCIPLE #2: READY-MADE FOODS DO NOT REQUIRE A COOKBOOK

With respect to this second principle, I absolutely get it. A cookbook is an adventure. It shouldn't be a walk around your own block. So, no—I don't use very many commercially produced ingredients. I'm a believer in the idea that it's important to know what's in your food. How much sugar? How much salt? Can you pronounce every ingredient? The best way to do this, of course, is to make it yourself. But I also know that it's unrealistic to make every ingredient from scratch, especially within the 5-ingredient concept. So, yes—I do use some commercially made products. When I do it's because it's a fairly complicated ingredient, like red curry paste. Or in the case of something like teriyaki sauce, I include a 5-ingredient DIY in the last chapter so that you can—should you be inclined—create it yourself.

MAKING THE MOST OF YOUR INGREDIENTS

One of the tricks to good vegan cooking is capturing the most flavor—and the most nutrition—from the ingredients. Vegan cooking with flavor isn't hard to do, but if you're used to cooking with animal-based products, there will be a small learning curve. We're so accustomed to being satiated with the siren's call of butter and cheese. I promise though that slow-cooked, browned onions and toasted tomato paste will knock your socks off! You've just got to be willing to work the flavor out of your ingredients. It takes a little bit more time but it's so much better for you in the long run.

LET'S TALK TIMING

Believe it or not, I actually polled my friends on this one and the responses were mixed. Most home chefs (myself among them) find a designated cooking time to be pretty arbitrary. What takes one person 30 minutes may take another an hour. So, I decided not to include cook times down to the minute. Rather, I chose two icons to indicate the fastest recipes in the book and the ones that require some prep ahead of time:

 These recipes are quick and easy. Generally speaking, you should have these dishes finished in about 30 to 45 minutes without a lot of cleanup fuss. Some of these are full meals, while others are sauces, salads or sides.

 If a recipe includes this icon, it means that there is a hands-off step that must be done in advance. For example, my 2-Step Overnight Oats (page 62) require a night in the refrigerator.

It is my hope that you find this cookbook to be inspirational. One of my goals, in addition to providing simple, healthy vegan recipes, was to take you on a culinary trip around the world. I wanted you to see that you could experience new and different flavors without breaking the bank or traveling to two or three different specialty markets. I also wanted to show you that extraordinary meals can be created with a limited number of ingredients that do not compromise our personal health, the health of our planet or the creatures with whom we coexist.

Thank you all for sharing this vegan journey with me.

EASY EVENING
EATS

I absolutely love this collection of recipes. It's wonderfully diverse in flavor—celebrating many cuisines from India to Asia to Italy, vegan style. I wanted these recipes to be simple in the selection of ingredients, but creative and complex in taste. You'll find everything from dishes using traditional pasta, like Penne alla Vodka (page 17), to those that use less common grains—like farro and lentils—in dishes like Easy Red Lentil Dal (page 22) and my Weeknight Grain Bowls with Chickpeas & Roasted Broccolini (page 42). There's something in here to please everyone, I promise!

Simple **SNOW PEAS** with Red Curry Coconut Broth

This simple Thai-inspired dish is perfect for cozying up on a chilly evening. It's both spicy and sweet—products of the red curry paste and creamy coconut milk. I chose snow peas as the vegetable because I love their crunch and their brilliant green color against the red curry broth. Like curry powder (see my Easy Red Lentil Dal on page 22), red curry paste is an easy single ingredient that brings a lot of flavor to a dish. Red curry is moderately spicy and slightly sweet, getting its flavor from red chilies. Other ingredients in red curry paste include garlic, galangal (Thai ginger), coriander, cumin, black pepper, kaffir lime leaves, lemongrass and turmeric. It's a complicated ingredient to make yourself, so I often opt for the store-bought version. Just pay attention when purchasing, as curry paste traditionally includes shrimp paste. There are vegan versions of red curry paste available though. I recommend Thai Kitchen's Red Curry Paste.

1 cup (185 g) dry jasmine rice

1 tbsp (14 g) coconut oil (see Recipe Notes)

1 tbsp (9 g) minced garlic (see Recipe Notes)

1 tbsp (6 g) minced fresh ginger (see Recipe Notes)

1 (4-oz [113-g]) jar red curry paste

2 (14-oz [414-ml]) cans full-fat, unsweetened coconut milk

2 tbsp (30 ml) tamari sauce

2 cups (126 g) fresh snow peas, washed with the ends trimmed

¼ cup (32 g) toasted cashews, roughly chopped (optional)

1 lime, cut into wedges (optional)

Prepare the jasmine rice according to the package directions.

Add the coconut oil to a large, deep-sided skillet. Turn the burner on to medium and heat the oil until shimmering. Add the garlic and ginger and sauté on medium-low heat until fragrant, 1 to 2 minutes.

Stir in the red curry paste and increase the heat to medium. Briefly toast the curry paste until fragrant, 2 to 3 minutes.

Add the coconut milk and tamari sauce. Bring to a simmer. Add the snow peas to the coconut milk broth. Cook until the peas become bright green.

Serve immediately over the jasmine rice. Top with the cashews and lime, if desired.

RECIPE NOTES

Coconut oil has a wonderful flavor and a low smoke point. An oil's smoke point is the temperature at which the oil starts to break down. This occurs at 350°F (175°C) for coconut oil. When cooking with it, be sure to monitor the heat of the pan to prevent the oil from smoking.

Two large cloves of garlic are about equal to 1 tablespoon (9 g) of minced garlic.

A thumb-sized piece of fresh ginger is about equal to 1 tablespoon (6 g) of minced ginger.

PENNE alla Vodka

SERVES

4

I used to wonder why cooks took the extra step of adding vodka to a tomato sauce. Was it worth all the fuss? As it turns out, the answer is yes. Taste vodka sauce next to any other tomato sauce and you'll immediately notice that vodka sauce is more complex and flavorful. I made this savory sauce vegan-friendly by swapping out Parmesan cheese for a couple tablespoons (10 g) of nutritional yeast and traditional heavy cream for coconut milk. Don't worry, as the coconut milk cooks alongside the acidic tomato paste, the coconut flavor mellows out, leaving just a hint of sweetness.

3 tbsp (45 ml) extra-virgin olive oil

1 cup (160 g) yellow onion, finely chopped

1 tsp salt

1 tbsp (9 g) minced garlic (See Recipe Note)

5 oz (142 g) tomato paste

¼ cup (60 ml) vodka

5 oz (148 ml) full-fat, unsweetened coconut milk

2 tbsp (10 g) nutritional yeast

1 lb (454 g) penne pasta

Fresh basil, torn (optional)

Add the olive oil to a large, deep-sided skillet. Turn the burner on to medium and heat the oil until shimmering. Add the onion and salt and reduce the heat to medium-low. Sauté the onion until it becomes golden brown, 12 to 15 minutes. Add the garlic and continue to sauté for 1 to 2 minutes.

Add the tomato paste and increase the heat to medium. Sauté the tomato paste until it becomes dark red, 2 to 3 minutes.

Remove the sauce from the heat and add the vodka, coconut milk and nutritional yeast. Stir until combined and return the pan to the burner. Bring to a simmer and allow the vodka to cook off, about 30 minutes.

Cook the pasta in accordance with the package directions. Reserve 1 cup (240 ml) of pasta water. It can be used to thin the vodka sauce if necessary. If the sauce becomes too thick, add the pasta water ¼ cup (60 ml) at a time.

Add the cooked pasta directly into the finished sauce and stir to coat. Season with fresh basil, if desired.

RECIPE NOTE

Two large cloves of garlic are about equal to 1 tablespoon (9 g) of minced garlic.

BUTTERNUT SQUASH GNOCCHI
with Browned Butter Sauce & Crispy Sage

SERVES
2

I often call dishes like this one "first date food." Imagine, if you will, that you've met someone you really, really like and you want to cook them dinner for the first time. Maybe you want to spend the rest of your life with them. Then you discover that they are vegan. You panic—how do you impress someone with your cooking when meat, cream, eggs and cheese are off the table? This recipe will get your relationship headed in the right direction, I promise. Just don't forget to send me an invitation to the wedding.

2 small butternut squash
(see Recipe Notes)

¼ cup (60 ml) + 2 tbsp
(30 ml) extra-virgin olive oil,
divided

¼ cup (6 g) fresh sage

1 tbsp (7 g) flaxseed meal

2½ cups (312 g) all-purpose
flour + more as needed

1 tbsp (18 g) + 1 tsp salt,
divided

½ cup (114 g) vegan butter
(see Recipe Notes)

1 tbsp (9 g) minced garlic
(see Recipe Notes)

2 tsp (10 ml) fresh lemon juice

⅛ tsp pepper

Preheat the oven to 350°F (175°C).

Wash the butternut squash and trim each end to create a flat surface. Place the squash upright on one of the trimmed ends and slice in half lengthwise.

Place the squash cut side down on a large baking sheet. Add enough water to the baking sheet to submerge the bottom of the squash. Lightly baste the rest of the squash with 1 tablespoon (15 ml) of the olive oil. This will prevent the skin from burning. Roast the squash for about 30 minutes until it is easily pierced with a fork.

While the squash is roasting, heat a small skillet and add 1 tablespoon (15 ml) of the olive oil and heat until shimmering. Add the sage and sauté until crispy, 1 to 2 minutes. Set aside.

Combine the flaxseed meal with 3 tablespoons (45 ml) of water. Mix thoroughly and set aside for 5 minutes. The flaxseed will thicken and take on a gelatinous consistency. This is often called a flaxseed egg.

Line a baking sheet with parchment paper.

Allow the squash to cool. Scoop out the seeds and discard. Remove the meat of the squash and combine it with ¼ cup (60 ml) of olive oil, the flaxseed egg, flour and 1 teaspoon of salt. Using your hands, combine the ingredients until a dough forms. If the dough is too sticky, add more flour 1 tablespoon (8 g) at a time. If it is too dry, add more water 1 tablespoon (15 ml) at a time. Do not overhandle the dough.

On a lightly floured surface, roll the dough out into 18-inch (46-cm)-long ropes about 2 inches (5 cm) in diameter. Using a sharp knife, cut the dough into 1-inch (2.5-cm) pieces and set each piece on the parchment paper. When you've cut all of the gnocchi, allow it to sit for about 1 hour to dry.

In a large stockpot, bring 4 quarts (3.8 L) of water and 1 tablespoon (18 g) of the salt to a boil. Add the gnocchi in small batches and cook for 4 to 6 minutes. The gnocchi should float to the top when cooked. Return the cooked gnocchi to the baking sheet.

Add the butter to a large, deep-sided stockpot. Turn the burner on medium-low until the butter is melted. Add the garlic and sauté until fragrant, about 1 minute. Add the gnocchi and sauté until browned. Add the lemon juice.

Serve immediately with the crispy sage and pepper to taste.

RECIPE NOTES

To save time, you can use frozen butternut squash. You will need to use additional flour due to the moisture content in frozen squash. I recommend starting with an additional ¼ cup (32 g) of flour and adding 1 tablespoon (8 g) at a time as necessary.

The type of vegan butter used in this recipe matters. Oil-based vegan butters and buttery spreads won't brown. Instead, choose a nut-based butter.

Two large cloves of garlic are about equal to 1 tablespoon (9 g) of minced garlic.

SERVES
2

LEMON-GARLIC PASTA
with Simple Spring Vegetables

This vegan dinner may seem involved, but it's super easy. Vibrant veggies accented with a fresh, lemon-garlic sauce give this dish a ton of flavor. The breadcrumbs add the perfect amount of salty crunchiness. I highly recommend making your own breadcrumbs for this dish. It's a simple task and a good way to use up those pesky bread heels that no one seems to want to eat. If you decide not to make your own, look for fresh breadcrumbs in your grocery store's bakery section.

1 bunch asparagus, washed and trimmed

1 lb (454 g) trumpet pasta (see Recipe Notes)

3 tbsp (45 ml) extra-virgin olive oil, divided

1 tbsp (9 g) minced garlic (see Recipe Notes)

½ cup (54 g) Italian breadcrumbs (or make your own using the recipe on page 141)

½ pint (150 g) grape tomatoes, washed and sliced in half

2 tbsp (30 ml) fresh lemon juice

Lemon zest, to taste

Fresh basil, torn

Set a steamer basket in a large stockpot with 1 to 2 inches (2.5 to 5 cm) of water. Bring the water to a boil and add the asparagus. Steam for 4 to 6 minutes, until the asparagus is bright green. You want to maintain a crisp texture. Rinse the asparagus with cold water to stop the cooking process and cut it into bite-size pieces. Set aside.

Cook the pasta according to the package directions.

Add 1 tablespoon (15 ml) of olive oil to a large, deep-sided skillet. Turn the burner on to medium and heat until shimmering. Add the garlic, reduce the heat to medium-low and sauté until fragrant, about 1 minute. Be careful not to burn the garlic, as it will become bitter. Add the breadcrumbs and toast until golden brown. Remove the breadcrumbs and wipe out the pan.

Add the remaining 2 tablespoons (30 ml) of olive oil and heat until shimmering. Add the asparagus and tomatoes and sauté for 1 to 2 minutes until the tomatoes just begin to soften. Add the pasta and the lemon juice. Toss to coat and heat until warmed through. Serve immediately topped with the lemon zest, breadcrumbs and basil.

RECIPE NOTES

No steamer basket? No problem! You can steam asparagus in the microwave. To do this, wrap the trimmed asparagus in damp paper towels and microwave on high for 3 minutes. Just be careful removing it from the microwave. The steam will be very hot!

I chose trumpet pasta for this recipe, but don't be afraid to swap it out. Look for a pasta shape with lots of nooks to host those homemade breadcrumbs.

Two large cloves of garlic are about equal to 1 tablespoon (9 g) of minced garlic.

Easy Red Lentil **DAL**

If you're not familiar with dal, you're in for a treat! *Dal* is a general term for a stew made by simmering lentils until they become soft. I like making red lentil dal the most. Red lentils are mild in flavor and break down when cooked, creating a savory stew that tastes as good on its own as it does over a bowl of basmati rice. Dals are seasoned differently, but for the sake of an easy dinner, this one uses just one spice (or spice blend): curry powder. Curry powder is a combination of turmeric, chili powder, coriander, cumin and ginger in just the right proportions to create a warm, savory vegan meal.

1 tbsp (14 g) coconut oil
(see Recipe Notes)

1 cup (160 g) yellow onion,
finely chopped

1 tsp salt

1 tbsp (9 g) minced garlic
(see Recipe Notes)

1 tbsp (6 g) minced ginger
(see Recipe Notes)

2 tbsp (32 g) tomato paste

1 tbsp (6 g) curry powder

1 cup (192 g) red lentils,
rinsed with any debris
removed

1 (14-oz [414-ml]) can
full-fat, unsweetened
coconut milk

½ cup (8 g) cilantro, washed
and torn (optional)

Add the coconut oil to a large stockpot. Turn the burner to medium and heat until shimmering. Add the onion and the salt and sauté on medium-low heat until the onion becomes golden brown, 12 to 15 minutes. Add the garlic and ginger and sauté until fragrant, 1 to 2 minutes.

Add the tomato paste and increase the heat to medium. Sauté until the tomato paste becomes dark red, 2 to 3 minutes. Add the curry powder and stir to combine. Sauté until fragrant, about 1 minute.

Add the lentils and stir to coat. Add 1 cup (240 ml) of water and the coconut milk. Bring to a simmer and cook, covered, until the lentils are soft, about 20 minutes. If the lentils become too dry, add additional water ½ cup (120 ml) at a time.

Serve the lentils with the cilantro, if desired.

RECIPE NOTES

Coconut oil has a wonderful flavor and a low smoke point. An oil's smoke point is the temperature at which the oil starts to break down. This occurs at 350°F (175°C) for coconut oil. When cooking with it, be sure to monitor the heat of the pan to prevent the oil from smoking.

Two large cloves of garlic are about equal to 1 tablespoon (9 g) of minced garlic.

A thumb-sized piece of fresh ginger is about equal to 1 tablespoon (6 g) of minced ginger.

One-Pot Sun-Dried Tomato & Chickpea **STEW**

SERVES
2

This dinner ranks up there among my favorites. Not only is it really rich and savory, I almost always have all of the ingredients in my kitchen, making it an easy answer to the late-afternoon question: "What's for dinner?" This recipe uses one of my favorite kitchen hacks—sautéing tomato paste for extra flavor. You'll see this again and again throughout my recipes, and for good reason. Sautéing tomato paste gives it an amazing richness. I've made this recipe with both dried and canned chickpeas. For the sake of ease, I recommend using canned chickpeas.

1 (8-oz [227-g]) jar sun-dried tomatoes, packed in oil

½ cup (80 g) yellow onion, chopped

¾ tsp salt

1 tbsp (9 g) minced garlic (see Recipe Notes)

1 tbsp (3 g) Italian seasoning (see Recipe Notes)

¼ cup (66 g) tomato paste

1 (25-oz [708-g]) can chickpeas, drained and rinsed

1 (14-oz [397-g]) can diced tomatoes

⅛ tsp pepper

Fresh basil (optional)

Drain the sun-dried tomatoes, reserving 1 tablespoon (15 ml) of the oil.

Add 1 tablespoon (15 ml) of the reserved oil to a large skillet. Turn the burner to medium and heat until the oil is shimmering. Add the onion and salt and reduce the heat to medium-low. Sauté the onion until it becomes golden brown, 12 to 15 minutes.

Add the garlic and Italian seasoning and sauté for 1 to 2 minutes. Add the tomato paste and increase the heat to medium. Sauté the tomato paste until it turns dark red, 2 to 3 minutes.

Add the chickpeas, ½ cup (120 ml) of water, tomatoes and pepper. Reduce the heat and simmer until the chickpeas become soft, 20 to 25 minutes. Using a wooden spoon, gently mash some of the chickpeas and break the sun-dried tomatoes apart. Season with basil, if desired.

RECIPE NOTES

This dish is wonderful on its own, but if you're looking for a heartier meal, serve it over my Painless Polenta (page 45).

Two large cloves of garlic are about equal to 1 tablespoon (9 g) of minced garlic.

You may think it's cheating to use Italian seasoning, but I'm a big fan of herb and spice blends. Word on the street is that blends are often a way for herb and spice manufacturers to sell the dregs of their supply, so I do make an effort to shop high-quality brands. My favorite: Spice Jungle (www.spicejungle.com). The problem with a drawer full of individual spices is one of economy; they take up a lot of space, they can be costly and they don't last forever. The longer herbs and spices sit in your drawer, the less potent they become. It just makes sense to use blends.

Savory Root Vegetable **STEW**

SERVES
4

This simple stew is so flavorful. You'll be amazed that it is 100% vegan. I take the time to eke as much out of the vegetables as I can, which lends itself to layers upon layers of flavor. The trick to this recipe, though, is the combination of sautéed tomato paste, tamari sauce and maple syrup, which mimics a warm bacon sauce. As you may know, many beef stews start with bacon, so I wanted to capture that savory flavor in an easy, cruelty-free way. I use turnips in this version, but you can use any combination of root vegetables. I like to serve my vegetable stew over my Painless Polenta (page 45).

20–25 cremini mushrooms, washed and cut into even-sized wedges (see Recipe Notes)

3 tbsp (45 ml) olive oil, divided

2 cups (320 g) yellow onions, chopped

1 tsp salt

1 tbsp (9 g) minced garlic (see Recipe Notes)

¼ cup (66 g) tomato paste

¼ cup (60 ml) tamari sauce

2 tbsp (30 ml) maple syrup

3 carrots, washed and thickly sliced

1 lb (454 g) turnips, parsnips or other root vegetables, washed and cut into equal-sized pieces

⅛ tsp fresh ground pepper

In a large stockpot, add the mushrooms and ¼ cup (60 ml) of water. Simmer the mushrooms in the water until the water has almost cooked off. Add 1 tablespoon (15 ml) of the olive oil and sauté until the mushrooms are just beginning to brown, 3 to 5 minutes. Remove the mushrooms from the pot.

Add the remaining 2 tablespoons (30 ml) of olive oil to the stockpot and heat until shimmering. Add the onions and salt and reduce the heat to low. Cover the stockpot and allow the onions to cook for 10 minutes. They will soften and become translucent. Then, remove the cover and continue to slow cook the onions for an additional 10 to 15 minutes, stirring occasionally. They will turn a rich brown color. Then, add the garlic and continue to cook for 1 to 2 additional minutes.

Add the tomato paste and increase the heat to medium. Sauté the tomato paste until it becomes a dark red, 2 to 3 minutes. Add the tamari sauce and maple syrup and continue sautéing for 1 to 2 minutes. The maple syrup should begin to thicken.

Add the mushrooms, carrots, turnips and 1 cup (240 ml) of water to the pot. Stir to combine. Simmer, covered, for 30 to 35 minutes, stirring occasionally, until the root vegetables are easily pierced with a fork. The broth should have cooked down to a thick sauce. If the sauce is too thin, continue to simmer, uncovered, for about 5 minutes.

Serve with the fresh ground pepper.

RECIPE NOTES

You may be wondering why I simmer mushrooms in water before sautéing them in oil. This extra step causes the internal structure of the mushrooms to collapse. When oil is added later, the mushrooms will cook more quickly and absorb less of the oil.

Two large cloves of garlic are about equal to 1 tablespoon (9 g) of minced garlic.

Teriyaki Tofu & Asparagus **NOODLE BOWL**

There is nothing I love more than a dish that combines the salty-sweetness of teriyaki with the chewy deliciousness of ramen noodles—especially one that comes together with so few ingredients! In addition to those two flavors, this dish includes crispy-on-the-outside and soft-on-the-inside roasted tofu. It's the perfect vehicle for teriyaki sauce. I chose asparagus as the vegetable for its tender texture and brilliant green color. This vegan bowl is truly slurp-worthy!

2 (10-oz [283-g]) packages extra-firm tofu

2 tbsp (30 ml) safflower oil, divided

1 package rice ramen noodles (4 "cakes")

2 bunches fresh asparagus, washed with ends trimmed

2 scallions, washed and sliced with the white parts separated from the green parts

1 tbsp (9 g) minced garlic (see Recipe Note)

1 cup (240 ml) vegan teriyaki sauce (store-bought or homemade recipe on page 138)

Sriracha sauce, for extra spice (optional)

White sesame seeds, for aesthetics (optional)

Press the tofu for about 20 minutes to remove the water. This will allow the tofu to become crispy when cooked. You can press tofu by slicing each block in half and lining paper towels under, in between and on top of the stacked slabs to absorb the water. To aid in this process, I recommend putting a cutting board on top of the tofu blocks and weighing it down with something heavy, like a cast-iron skillet. This works, but I prefer using a tofu press—it's less messy and saves a lot of paper towels.

Preheat the oven to 425°F (220°C).

Cut the pressed tofu into 1-inch (2.5-cm) cubes. Using a basting brush, coat the baking sheet with a tablespoon (15 ml) of safflower oil, creating a thin layer. Lay the tofu cubes out on the baking sheet, keeping each piece separate. Roast the tofu for 20 minutes, flipping after 10 minutes.

While the tofu is baking, prepare the rice noodles according to the package directions. Cook to al dente, then rinse with cold water to stop the cooking process.

Steam the asparagus for 4 to 6 minutes, until tender. Rinse with cold water and cut into bite-size pieces.

Add the remaining tablespoon (15 ml) of safflower oil to a large, deep-sided skillet. Turn the burner to medium-low and heat until shimmering. Add the whites of the scallions and garlic. Sauté for 1 minute.

Add the baked tofu and the teriyaki sauce to the skillet. Gently stir to coat. Add the asparagus and cooked rice noodles. Heat through.

Serve immediately, topping with the scallion greens. Garnish with the Sriracha and sesame seeds, if desired.

RECIPE NOTE

Two large cloves of garlic are about equal to 1 tablespoon (9 g) of minced garlic.

SERVES
4

PASTA CARBONARA with Shiitake Mushroom "Bacon"

Pasta Carbonara is perhaps the ultimate comfort food. Traditionally, it is a bacon-and-egg dish. Eggs are used to create the creamy white sauce that coats the thick fettuccini noodles, while bacon gives the dish a savory, smoky taste. Believe it or not, these flavors are easy to replicate vegan-style. Shiitake mushrooms are roasted in a tamari–maple syrup sauce—mimicking the flavor of maple-smoked bacon—while blended creamy cashews create the deliciously decadent sauce.

1 cup (146 g) cashews

¼ cup (60 ml) tamari sauce

2 tbsp (30 ml) maple syrup

20–25 shiitake mushrooms, washed and sliced into ¼-inch (6-mm) pieces

1 tbsp (15 ml) safflower oil

1 lb (454 g) fettuccini pasta

2 tbsp (30 ml) fresh lemon juice

2 tbsp (10 g) nutritional yeast

1 clove garlic

1 tsp salt

Fresh ground pepper, to taste

Fresh parsley (optional)

Soak the cashews in 2 cups (480 ml) of just-boiling water for 30 minutes.

While the cashews are soaking, combine the tamari sauce and maple syrup. Lay the shiitake mushrooms out in a shallow dish and pour the tamari-maple mixture over the mushrooms. Set aside for 30 minutes.

Preheat the oven to 400°F (205°C).

Coat a small baking sheet with the safflower oil. Drain the marinade from the mushrooms and spread the mushrooms out on the baking sheet. Roast for 20 minutes, flipping the mushrooms after 10 minutes.

Cook the pasta according to the package directions. Reserve ¾ cup (180 ml) of the pasta water.

Drain and rinse the cashews. Combine the cashews, reserved pasta water, lemon juice, nutritional yeast, garlic and salt in a high-speed blender. Blend until creamy.

Toss the pasta with the cashew sauce and shiitake mushrooms. Season with the pepper and garnish with the parsley, if desired.

RECIPE NOTE

This dish is best served immediately. If you want to make it in advance, prep the pasta, cashew cream sauce and mushrooms separately. Reheat the pasta by running it under hot water. Reheat the mushrooms in the oven and warm the cashew cream sauce by re-blending it in your high-speed blender.

MAKES

2 PIZZAS

Time-Saving **TORTILLA PIZZA** with BBQ Jackfruit

In my house, tortilla pizzas are a popular menu item. The kids love them because they're tasty, and I love them because they're a simple way to pull together a meal with just a few ingredients. And a thin, crispy crust? That's easy to achieve using flour tortillas. We'll often do vegan-friendly tortilla tomato pies with a drizzle of olive oil and plenty of roasted vegetables. Here, I showcase my answer to BBQ chicken pizza by replacing chicken with a very convincing jackfruit substitute.

2 (15-oz [425-g]) cans young jackfruit, drained and rinsed

2 tbsp (30 ml) safflower oil

1½ cups (360 ml) vegan BBQ sauce, divided

2 (10-inch [25-cm]) flour tortillas

¼ red onion, sliced thin

¼ cup (4 g) fresh cilantro, washed and torn

Fresh cracked pepper, to taste

Chipotle Ranch Dressing (page 145; optional)

Preheat the oven to 400°F (205°C).

Using a knife and two forks, cut the jackfruit into small chunks and pull the pieces apart with the tines of the forks. It should have the same appearance as shredded pork.

Wrap the pulled jackfruit in a clean kitchen towel and squeeze to remove excess water. If the jackfruit is too wet when it goes into the pan, it will steam rather than crisp.

Add the safflower oil to a large skillet. Turn the burner to medium and heat until shimmering. Add the dried jackfruit and sauté on medium heat until the jackfruit begins to crisp on the outside. Add 1 cup (240 ml) of the BBQ sauce and continue to sauté, allowing the sauce to thicken and caramelize, 3 to 5 minutes. Remove from the heat.

Spread the remaining ½ cup (120 ml) of BBQ sauce on the tortillas. Top with the jackfruit and sliced red onion. Bake until the tortillas are crispy, about 6 minutes.

Top with the cilantro, cracked pepper and Chipotle Ranch Dressing, if desired.

SERVES
2

30-Minute Shiitake Mushroom & Bok Choy
RAMEN NOODLE BOWLS

Noodle bowls are all the rage these days and they're very easy to adapt to a vegan diet. Miso paste, made from fermented soybeans, is the key to this simple meal. Miso paste is the whole package—it's savory, sweet, tangy and salty. It's also packed with probiotics and protein. I like to add chewy, al dente rice ramen noodles, sautéed shiitake mushrooms and mustardy bok choy to my bowl.

12–15 shiitake mushrooms, stems trimmed and sliced in ¼-inch (6-mm) pieces (see Recipe Notes)

2 tbsp (30 ml) safflower oil, divided

1 tbsp (9 g) minced garlic (see Recipe Notes)

1 tbsp (6 g) minced ginger (see Recipe Notes)

¼ cup (60 ml) tamari sauce

2 rice ramen noodle "cakes"

2 heads bok choy, washed and trimmed

½ cup (130 g) yellow miso paste

Sriracha sauce, to taste (optional)

Add the shiitake mushrooms and ¼ cup (60 ml) of water to a large stockpot. Simmer the mushrooms until the water has almost cooked off, 3 to 5 minutes. When a small amount of water remains, add 1 tablespoon (15 ml) of the safflower oil. Continue to sauté the mushrooms until they start to brown, about 2 minutes. Set aside.

Add the remaining tablespoon (15 ml) of safflower oil to the stockpot. Turn the burner to medium and heat until shimmering. Add the garlic and ginger and sauté on medium-low heat until fragrant, about 1 to 2 minutes. Add the tamari sauce and 7½ cups (1.8 L) of water. Simmer for 10 minutes.

While the broth is simmering, prepare the rice noodles according to the package directions. Drain the noodles when they are al dente and rinse with cold water to stop the cooking process.

Add the bok choy to the broth and remove the broth from the heat.

In a small bowl, combine the miso paste with ½ cup (120 ml) of warm water and whisk vigorously until the miso paste is dissolved. Add the miso slurry to the broth. Add the mushrooms to the broth.

Serve immediately by placing the desired amount of noodles in the bottom of your serving bowls. Top with the broth and add sriracha sauce for additional heat, if desired.

RECIPE NOTES

You may be wondering why I simmer mushrooms in water before sautéing them in oil. This extra step causes the internal structure of the mushrooms to collapse. When oil is added later, the mushrooms will cook more quickly and absorb less of the oil.

Two large cloves of garlic are about equal to 1 tablespoon (9 g) of minced garlic.

A thumb-sized piece of fresh ginger is about equal to 1 tablespoon (6 g) of minced ginger.

PORTOBELLO MUSHROOM "STEAKS"
with Easy Cauliflower Mash and Roasted Broccolini

Move over traditional meat-and-potatoes! This simple vegan dish uses very few ingredients but makes a complete meal full of wonderful, healthy vegetables. Roasted portobello mushrooms take the place of steak, while creamy cauliflower mash offers a healthy twist on mashed potatoes.

1 head garlic

3 tbsp (45 ml) extra-virgin olive oil, divided

1 cup (146 g) cashews

2 heads cauliflower, washed and cut into large florets

4 portobello mushrooms

1½ tsp (9 g) salt, divided + more to taste

⅛ tsp pepper + more to taste

2 bunches broccolini, washed and trimmed

1 tbsp (15 ml) fresh lemon juice

2 tbsp (10 g) nutritional yeast

Lemon zest, to taste

Preheat the oven to 400°F (205°C).

Cut the top quarter off the head of garlic, exposing the cloves. Wrap the garlic, cut side up, in aluminum foil. Drizzle 1 tablespoon (15 ml) of the olive oil over the garlic and close the foil over the top. Roast for 1 hour.

Soak the cashews in 2 cups (480 ml) of just-boiling water for 30 minutes. Set aside.

While the garlic is roasting, prepare the cauliflower. Arrange your steamer basket in a large stockpot with 1 to 2 inches (2.5 to 5 cm) of water. Bring to a boil. Add the cauliflower florets and steam for 6 minutes, or until easily pierced with a fork. Set aside.

Wash the portobello mushrooms and remove the stems. Soak the gills in warm water for about 1 minute to soften and then scoop out the gills using a spoon. Pat the mushrooms dry with a clean kitchen towel. Lay the caps in a shallow baking dish, gill side down, and drizzle with 1 tablespoon (15 ml) of the olive oil. Sprinkle with salt and pepper to taste. Set aside.

When the garlic has roasted for 50 minutes, toss the broccolini in 1 tablespoon (15 ml) of the olive oil, ½ teaspoon of the salt and ⅛ teaspoon of the pepper. Spread the broccolini on a large baking sheet and roast in the oven on the middle rack until it is charred, about 20 minutes.

When the broccolini has roasted for 10 minutes, remove the baking sheet from the oven and move the broccolini to one side of it, making room for the portobello mushrooms. Add the mushrooms to the baking sheet and roast in the oven for 6 minutes. Remove the mushrooms and set them aside to rest for 5 minutes. Continue roasting the broccolini for another 4 minutes.

When the garlic is finished roasting, set aside to cool. Drain and rinse the cashews.

When the garlic has cooled, carefully remove the cloves from the skin. In a high-speed blender, combine the cashews, ¾ cup (180 ml) of water, 1 teaspoon of salt, the roasted cloves of garlic, lemon juice and nutritional yeast. Blend until creamy.

Combine the steamed cauliflower and cashew cream sauce in a large bowl and mash with a potato masher until creamy.

Slice the portobello mushrooms and serve with the creamy mashed cauliflower and roasted broccolini on the side. Season with the salt, pepper and lemon zest, to taste.

30-Minute **ZUCCHINI NOODLES**
with Sun-Dried Tomato Pesto

SERVES
2

3 large zucchinis

1 tsp salt, divided

1 (8-oz [227-g]) jar sun-dried tomatoes, packed in oil

1 cup (24 g) fresh basil + additional for garnish

¼ cup (34 g) pine nuts (see Recipe Note)

2 tbsp (10 g) nutritional yeast

2 tbsp (30 ml) fresh lemon juice

½ tbsp (8 ml) extra-virgin olive oil + more as needed

This dish is a quick and easy go-to dinner at my house. It's a nice twist on traditional pasta and tomato sauce, with the zucchini noodles offering up an additional way to get more vegetables into my family's diet. Sun-dried tomato pesto might sound like it's fancy, but it comes together with just a few ingredients that can easily be found at the grocery store. When I make zucchini noodles, I prefer a pappardelle-style noodle because it allows for a little more crunch. I lightly salt the zucchini after I've spiralized it to draw out moisture, which allows it to maintain crispness.

Wash and spiralize the zucchini. Put the spiralized zucchini into a colander and sprinkle with ½ teaspoon of the salt. Toss the zucchini noodles to coat and allow to rest for 15 minutes. The salt will draw out some of the water.

While the zucchini is resting, drain the oil from the sun-dried tomatoes. Reserve ½ cup (120 ml) of the oil. If there isn't enough in the jar, you can supplement with extra-virgin olive oil.

Remove the basil leaves from the stems, wash them and pat them dry.

Gently toast the pine nuts in a small, dry skillet on medium heat for 2 to 3 minutes, until golden brown. This will add extra flavor to the sauce.

In a small food processor, combine the sun-dried tomatoes, reserved oil, basil, pine nuts, nutritional yeast, ½ teaspoon salt and lemon juice. Process until smooth.

Pat the zucchini noodles dry with a clean towel to remove excess water. Add the olive oil to a large skillet. Turn the burner to medium and heat until shimmering. Add the zucchini noodles and gently sauté until they are bright green, 1 to 2 minutes.

Add the sun-dried tomato pesto and heat until warmed through. Top with freshly torn basil.

RECIPE NOTE

Pine nuts are delicate and high in fat. This gives them a creamy consistency that adds richness to this dish. Because of the fat content they do burn quickly, so be sure to keep an eye on them as they're toasting.

Crispy **BAKED EGGPLANT**
with a Simple Homemade Tomato Sauce

SERVES
2

2 eggplants, washed and peeled

2 tsp (12 g) salt, divided

3 tbsp (21 g) flaxseed meal

2 cups (216 g) Italian breadcrumbs (homemade recipe on page 141)

3 tbsp (45 ml) safflower oil, divided

2 tbsp (30 ml) extra-virgin olive oil

½ cup (80 g) yellow onion, chopped

1 tbsp (9 g) minced garlic

2 tbsp (32 g) tomato paste

1 (28-oz [794-g]) can unsalted whole peeled tomatoes, juices reserved

Fresh basil, torn (optional)

RECIPE NOTE

If you would like the sauce a bit less chunky, I recommend using an immersion blender.

Naming this recipe proved to be a bit tricky. I wanted to call it Eggplant Parmesan, but since there's no Parmesan in it, I decided on Crispy Baked Eggplant with a Simple Homemade Tomato Sauce. While it's modeled on Eggplant Parmesan, it's a much healthier version. I swapped out the eggs in the breading for flaxseed meal—a vegan superfood. And it's baked instead of fried.

Slice the peeled eggplants into 1-inch (2.5-cm)-thick discs. Lay the sliced eggplant out on a clean kitchen towel and sprinkle with 1 teaspoon of the salt. Allow to rest for 15 minutes. The eggplant will start to shed its moisture.

While the eggplant is resting, in a small bowl, combine the flaxseed meal with ½ cup (120 ml) of water. Mix thoroughly and allow to rest for 5 minutes. The mixture will become gelatinous. This is often called a flaxseed egg.

Preheat the oven to 425°F (220°C).

Pour the flaxseed egg onto a plate (you will need room to spread it out so that you can dip the eggplant into it). Spread the breadcrumbs out on a second plate.

Prepare a baking sheet by spreading 1 tablespoon (15 ml) of the safflower oil on the sheet to create a thin layer of oil. Pat the eggplant dry and dip each piece of eggplant into the flaxseed egg, spreading it evenly over both sides. Press both sides of each piece into the breadcrumbs and then place the breaded eggplant on the baking sheet. Continue until all the eggplant is coated.

Drizzle the remaining 2 tablespoons (30 ml) of safflower oil over the top of the eggplant slices. Roast the eggplant for 35 to 40 minutes, flipping halfway through. The eggplant is done when the breadcrumbs become crispy and browned.

Add the olive oil to a large deep-sided skillet. Turn the burner to medium and heat until shimmering. Add the onion and remaining teaspoon of salt and reduce the heat to medium-low. Sauté the onion until golden brown, 12 to 15 minutes. Add the garlic and sauté for 1 to 2 minutes.

Increase the heat to medium and add the tomato paste. Sauté the tomato paste until it is a deep, rich red, 2 to 3 minutes. Add the tomatoes and ½ cup (120 ml) of the retained juices. Bring to a simmer. Simmer, covered, for 20 minutes. Gently crush the tomatoes with a wooden spoon.

Spoon the tomato sauce over the eggplant and serve with fresh basil, if desired. Vegan Parmesan is another great addition to this dish. You can find a recipe for it on page 134.

Weeknight **GRAIN BOWLS**
with Chickpeas & Roasted Broccolini

SERVES
2

This cozy grain bowl is the perfect vegan dinner option when the weather gets cool. Between the farro and chickpeas, it is packed with protein and fiber. The simple salt-and-pepper roasted broccolini adds a wonderful kick, but the real star of this dish is the ever-so-slightly sweet tahini dressing. If you're not familiar with tahini, it's a thick paste made from ground sesame seeds. It has a distinct, nutty flavor that comes alive with the addition of fresh lemon juice and extra-virgin olive oil.

1 cup (200 g) farro

1 (14-oz [397-g]) can chickpeas, drained and rinsed

2 bunches broccolini, trimmed

½ cup (120 ml) + 1 tbsp (15 ml) extra-virgin olive oil, divided

1 tsp salt, divided

¼ tsp pepper

½ cup (130 g) tahini

1 clove garlic

4 tbsp (60 ml) fresh lemon juice

½ tbsp (8 ml) maple syrup

Toasted Pumpkin Seeds (page 142; optional)

Preheat the oven to 375°F (190°C).

Spread the farro out on a baking sheet and toast in the oven for 10 minutes until the grains are fragrant and lightly browned. Remove the farro from the baking sheet and combine with 3 cups (720 ml) of water in a second saucepan. Bring to a simmer and cook, covered, for 35 to 45 minutes, until the farro is slightly chewy.

In a medium-sized saucepan, add the chickpeas and enough water to cover them. Bring to a simmer and cover. Allow the chickpeas to simmer until softened, about 25 minutes.

Increase the oven temperature to 400°F (205°C).

While the chickpeas and farro are cooking, spread the trimmed broccolini out on the baking sheet. Toss with 1 tablespoon (15 ml) of the olive oil, ½ teaspoon of the salt and the pepper. Roast until the broccolini is slightly charred.

In a high-speed blender, combine the tahini, ½ cup (120 ml) of olive oil, garlic, ½ teaspoon of salt, lemon juice and maple syrup. Blend until creamy. If the dressing is too thick, add cold water 1 tablespoon (15 ml) at a time. I usually need to add 2 to 4 tablespoons (30 to 60 ml) of water.

Serve by filling each bowl with the farro, chickpeas and roasted broccolini. Drizzle with the tahini dressing and top with the Toasted Pumpkin Seeds, if using.

Painless **POLENTA**

MAKES
APPROXIMATELY
4 CUPS (740 G)

1 (14-oz [420-ml]) can
full-fat, unsweetened
coconut milk

1 cup (156 g) polenta

1 tsp salt

2 tbsp (10 g) nutritional
yeast

I used to think making polenta was more trouble than it was worth. Then I made it. If you're not familiar with polenta, it's a coarsely ground cornmeal. When slow cooked in water and (in this case) coconut milk, it becomes a creamy magical backdrop to all things savory, like my One-Pot Sun-Dried Tomato & Chickpea Stew (page 25). If you're feeling ambitious, you can let cooked polenta set in the refrigerator and panfry polenta cakes, then top them with a rich, slow-roasted tomato compote (see my blog for the deets on this). I digress . . . the point is, this dish is absolutely worth making. Every time.

In a medium-sized saucepan, bring the coconut milk and 1½ cups (360 ml) of water to a simmer. Slowly add the polenta, stirring constantly. Add the salt and nutritional yeast and reduce to a low simmer. Cover and cook for 20 minutes, stirring every 5 minutes.

When the polenta becomes too thick to stir, add more water ½ cup (120 ml) at a time. You will likely need to add about 2 cups (480 ml) of additional water. The polenta is done when it is smooth and creamy and no longer gritty and sand-like in texture.

RECIPE NOTE

Polenta is best served immediately. After sitting for a time it will become thick and lumpy. I try and time it to be done just as the other elements of my meal are wrapping up. Of course, things don't always go according to plan in the kitchen. If this happens to you, warm it up on the stove by adding some additional water—start with ¼ cup (60 ml)—and whisk vigorously.

STRAIGHT-FORWARD SOUPS *and* SALADS

Soups and salads are two of my favorite food categories! I love a good, hearty bowl of soup when the weather is cool—and even when it's not. Recipes like my Easy Butternut Squash Soup (page 48) make me feel all warm and cozy. My Simple Miso Soup (page 59) is a great option when I'm tired and hungry and just want something warm on the table in the shortest amount of time. My salads are equally hearty, packed with fiber-rich chickpeas and nutty, chewy farro to make them filling. I finish them off with fresh herbs and greens for a ton of flavor.

Easy **BUTTERNUT SQUASH SOUP**

SERVES
4

To get as much flavor out of the vegetables and into this savory, autumn-appropriate soup, I take the extra time and really let the onion sweat. Slowly cooking them on low heat in coconut oil creates a lovely, natural sweetness. Coconut milk—the full-fat, unsweetened kind you find in a can—makes this savory soup so divine you'd never guess that it's dairy-free. Finally, adding just a touch of sherry vinegar livens up this soup without adding overpowering acidity.

5 lbs (2.3 kg) butternut squash

½ tbsp (8 ml) safflower oil

2 tbsp (28 g) coconut oil

1 cup (160 g) roughly chopped yellow onion

2 tsp (12 g) salt, divided

1 tbsp (9 g) roughly chopped garlic

½ tsp pumpkin pie spice

2–3 tbsp (30–45 ml) maple syrup (see Recipe Note)

1 (14-oz [414-ml]) can full-fat, unsweetened coconut milk, divided

1 tbsp (15 ml) sherry vinegar

Fresh ground pepper, to taste

Toasted Pumpkin Seeds (page 142; optional)

Preheat the oven to 350°F (175°C).

Wash the butternut squash and trim each end to create a flat surface. Place the squash upright on one of the trimmed ends and slice in half lengthwise.

Place the squash cut side down on a large baking sheet. Add enough water to submerge the bottom of the squash. Lightly baste the skin of the squash with the safflower oil. This will prevent the skin from burning. Roast the squash for about 40 minutes until it is easily pierced with a fork. Allow to cool.

When the squash has cooled, use a spoon to discard the seeds. Gently scoop the meat of the squash out of the skin and set aside. Discard the skins.

Add the coconut oil to a large stockpot. Turn the burner on to medium and heat until shimmering. Add the onion and 1 teaspoon of the salt. Reduce the heat to medium-low and sauté the onion for 10 minutes, covered. After 10 minutes, remove the cover and continue to slow cook the onion for another 20 minutes, stirring occasionally. The onion will turn a deep golden brown. Add the garlic and sauté for 1 to 2 minutes. Add the pumpkin pie spice and sauté until fragrant, about 1 minute. Add 2 tablespoons (30 ml) of the maple syrup and stir. Add the butternut squash, 1 cup (240 ml) of water and 10 ounces (296 ml) of the coconut milk. Increase the heat and simmer for 15 minutes.

Using an immersion blender, blend the soup until it is creamy. If it is too thick, add water ½ cup (120 ml) at a time.

Season with the remaining teaspoon of salt and additional maple syrup, if using. Add the sherry vinegar, pepper, remaining 4 ounces (118 ml) of coconut milk and Toasted Pumpkin Seeds, if desired. Serve immediately.

RECIPE NOTE

I like to add the maple syrup slowly and taste as I go. The sweetness of the butternut squash may vary from squash to squash and you want to avoid having this soup become too sweet.

One-Pot Asparagus & **WHITE BEAN SOUP**

Somewhat surprisingly, this simple soup is a family favorite. I say "surprisingly" because I have two young children and this soup is green. It's also wonderfully creamy. The coconut milk embraces the slight bitterness of the asparagus while the nutritional yeast gives this springtime dish a delicate cheesy flavor. The white beans thicken the soup while adding protein, fiber and iron.

2 large bunches fresh asparagus, washed and trimmed

1 tbsp (15 ml) extra-virgin olive oil

1 cup (160 g) roughly chopped yellow onion

1 tsp salt

1 tbsp (9 g) roughly chopped garlic (see Recipe Notes)

1 quart (960 ml) low-sodium vegetable broth

1 (14-oz [397-g]) can cannellini beans, drained and rinsed

1 (14-oz [414-ml]) can full-fat, unsweetened coconut milk

2 tbsp (10 g) nutritional yeast

1 tbsp (15 ml) fresh lemon juice

Fresh ground pepper, to taste

In a large stockpot fit with a steamer basket, add 1 to 2 inches (2.5 to 5 cm) of water and steam the asparagus for 5 to 7 minutes, until bright green. Rinse with cold water to stop the cooking process. Cut the tops from half of the asparagus and set aside for garnish.

Drain and dry the stockpot. Add the olive oil, turn the burner to medium and heat until shimmering. Reduce the heat to medium-low and add the onion and salt. Sauté until golden brown, 12 to 15 minutes. Add the garlic and sauté for 1 to 2 minutes.

Increase the heat to medium and add the vegetable broth, cooked asparagus, cannellini beans, coconut milk and nutritional yeast. Bring to a simmer and cook for about 15 minutes, until the beans are soft. Using an immersion blender, blend the soup until smooth and creamy.

Stir in the lemon juice and garnish with the asparagus tops and pepper. Serve immediately.

RECIPE NOTES

No steamer basket? No problem! You can steam asparagus in the microwave. To do this, wrap the trimmed asparagus in damp paper towels and microwave on high for 3 minutes. Just be careful removing it from the microwave. The steam will be very hot!

Two large cloves of garlic are about equal to 1 tablespoon (9 g) of minced garlic.

Roasted BEET & FARRO SALAD

SERVES
2

Hearty salads with healthy grains are a summertime favorite of mine. Farro is packed with protein and fiber and has a delicate nutty taste. If farro is toasted before it is cooked, it takes on a delightful chewy texture—perfect for the salad-as-a-meal option! I paired this with roasted beets, balsamic vinegar and fresh arugula. The sweetness of the beets contrasted with the peppery arugula and tangy balsamic makes this simple salad taste complex!

2 beets, thoroughly washed (I use both red and golden beets)

¼ cup (60 ml) + 1 tbsp (15 ml) extra-virgin olive oil, divided

Salt and pepper (8–10 generous twists of a salt and pepper mill)

1 cup (200 g) farro

¼ cup (34 g) hazelnuts

¼ cup (60 ml) balsamic vinegar

1 tsp fresh lemon juice

3 cups (60 g) loosely packed arugula

Lemon zest, to taste

Preheat the oven to 375°F (190°C).

Prepare a baking sheet with parchment paper or a silicone baking mat.

Trim the root and stem end of each beet. Slice the beets into quarters or halves to create even-sized pieces. Drizzle the beets with 1 tablespoon (15 ml) of the olive oil and sprinkle with the salt and pepper. Place them on the prepared baking sheet and roast for 1 hour on the middle rack. The beets are done when they can be easily pierced with a fork.

Spread the farro out on a small baking sheet. Toast in the oven with the beets for 10 minutes. Remove the farro from the oven and simmer in 3 cups (720 ml) of water until the farro is densely chewy, about 45 minutes. Allow to cool.

While the beets are roasting and the farro is cooking, spread the hazelnuts out on a small baking sheet. Roast them in the oven with the beets for 15 minutes. When the hazelnuts come out of the oven, place them on a clean kitchen towel and fold the towel over the nuts. Vigorously rub the hazelnuts between the fold to remove the skins. Allow to cool, then roughly chop them.

Prepare the dressing by combining ¼ cup (60 ml) of the olive oil, the balsamic vinegar and lemon juice.

Once the beets have cooled, peel the skin with your fingertips and cut them into bite-size pieces.

Prepare the salad by laying a bed of arugula topped with farro on each plate. Add the sliced beets, chopped hazelnuts and some lemon zest. Drizzle with the salad dressing and season with salt and pepper, to taste.

RECIPE NOTE

This salad has some time-consuming elements. To food prep, you can roast the beets and hazelnuts, cook the farro and make the dressing in advance.

Herby **CHICKPEA & ORZO SALAD**

SERVES
2

This hearty vegan salad is the perfect warm weather treat! It's best served cold with some fresh herbs. I chose fresh basil for this recipe, but don't be afraid to toss in other types if your local farmers' market has other herbs you like. In fact, this salad is a great way to utilize your haul from a Saturday morning veggie-stand binge. The inclusion of both orzo pasta and chickpeas gives this salad a robustness, while the red onion and English cucumber give it eye-appealing color. A zesty lemon juice dressing adds the final touch.

1 (14-oz [397-g]) can chickpeas, drained and rinsed (see Recipe Notes)

1 cup (170 g) dry orzo pasta

¼ cup (60 ml) extra-virgin olive oil

1 tbsp (15 ml) fresh lemon juice

½ red onion, finely chopped

1 English cucumber, diced (see Recipe Notes)

¼ cup (6 g) fresh basil, washed and torn

Fresh parsley and/or dill (optional)

Salt and pepper, to taste

Lemon zest, to taste

In a medium-sized saucepan, add the chickpeas and cover with water. Simmer until the chickpeas are tender, about 25 minutes. Rinse the chickpeas with cold water and refrigerate until ready for use.

Cook the orzo pasta according to the package directions. Chill in the refrigerator until ready for use.

Prepare the dressing by combining the olive oil and lemon juice.

Assemble the salad by combining the orzo pasta, chickpeas, red onion, cucumber and lemon dressing. Top with the basil and any other fresh herbs, if desired. Add the salt, pepper and lemon zest, to taste.

RECIPE NOTES

While you can use chickpeas directly from a can, I like to take the extra step of simmering them first as it makes them more tender.

If you're food prepping this salad, make the chickpeas and orzo pasta in advance. That way they'll have time to cool before you put it all together.

This recipe calls for an English cucumber. An English cucumber is a longer, slimmer version of the popular slicing cucumber. It's typically wrapped in plastic which eliminates the need for wax on the skin. The seeds are underdeveloped, making them less bitter than their counterparts. If you can't find an English cucumber, you can substitute a slicing cucumber. I recommend removing the skin before dicing it.

Vegan **CAPRESE SALAD** with Basil Pesto

Caprese salad is the salad of summer! Typically it's tomato slices and fresh mozzarella cheese topped with basil and a balsamic vinaigrette. This recipe preserves the richness of a caprese salad by replacing the mozzarella cheese with slices of avocado. I further elevate this traditional recipe by serving it on a thin layer of vegan pesto sauce. It's a tangy, fresh version that substitutes lemon juice and nutritional yeast for Parmesan cheese.

⅔ cup (89 g) pine nuts, divided (see Recipe Note)

1 cup (24 g) fresh basil leaves, washed + extra leaves for garnish

1 clove garlic

2 tbsp (10 g) nutritional yeast

1 tsp salt

½ cup (120 ml) extra-virgin olive oil

2 medium vine-ripened tomatoes

1 avocado

Salt and fresh ground pepper, to taste

Gently toast the pine nuts in a small, dry skillet on medium heat for 2 to 3 minutes, until they turn a golden brown. Toasting the nuts will add extra flavor to the pesto.

In a small food processor, combine ½ cup (68 g) of the pine nuts, basil, garlic, nutritional yeast and salt. Pulse until no large pieces remain. Stir in the olive oil.

Wash and slice the tomatoes. Slice the avocado.

Spread a thin layer of the basil pesto on a plate. Arrange the tomato and avocado slices on top of the pesto. Garnish with basil leaves and the remaining pine nuts. Season with salt and pepper.

RECIPE NOTE

Pine nuts are delicate and high in fat. This gives them a creamy consistency that adds richness to this dish. Because of the fat content they do burn quickly, so be sure to keep an eye on them as they're toasting.

Simple **MISO SOUP**

SERVES
2

Miso soup is such an easy and healthy hot lunch or early light dinner. I particularly like it in the winter after a day of skiing when I'm too tired to really cook but hot soup sounds amazing. If you're not familiar with miso paste, it is made of fermented soybeans. It's savory, sweet, salty and tangy all at once. A single ingredient with a ton of umami. It's also loaded with health benefits—it's a probiotic and a complete protein. For some extra color and nutrition, I add spinach and soft tofu to this simple broth, making this soup the perfect midwinter meal.

1 tbsp (15 ml) extra-virgin olive oil

½ tbsp (5 g) finely minced garlic

1 scallion, white parts finely minced and green parts thinly sliced, divided

½ tbsp (3 g) finely minced ginger

1 tbsp (15 ml) tamari sauce

5 oz (142 g) soft tofu, cut into bite-size cubes

2 cups (60 g) loosely packed baby spinach

¼ cup (65 g) yellow miso paste

Add the olive oil to a medium-sized stockpot. Turn the burner to medium and heat until shimmering. Reduce the heat to medium-low and add the garlic, whites of the scallion and ginger. Sauté until fragrant, 1 to 2 minutes.

Add 3½ cups (840 ml) of water and the tamari sauce to the pot. Bring to a simmer. Simmer for 5 minutes and then remove from the heat. Stir in the tofu and spinach.

Combine the yellow miso paste with ½ cup (120 ml) of water. Whisk vigorously until the miso paste has dissolved. Stir the miso slurry into the broth.

Serve immediately topped with the scallion greens.

The
MORNING RUSH
MADE EASY

Whether I'm rushing out the door for work or getting the kids to school (or both), breakfast is the meal that often falls by the wayside. I truly find it the hardest meal to balance. My food-starved brain wants to grab the first thing I lay my eyes on. If I'm not prepared, this ends up being the castaway crusts from my kids' toast and a cup of tea. Having small Mason jars of overnight oats in the refrigerator or the Grab & Go Banana Bread Muffin Tops on page 65 (because everyone knows the tops are the best part) helps me to stay on track.

2-Step **OVERNIGHT OATS**

SERVES

1

Overnight oats are a midlife "eureka!" idea for me. I didn't discover this concept until recently, and it's been a game changer. Before I discovered overnight oats, the word "oatmeal" conjured up images of that congealed mass that often greets you after a "breakfast included" hotel stay. So, if you're into thick, goopy, almost unidentifiable oatmeal, this recipe is probably not for you. On the other hand, if you like a sweet, slightly nutty and a little bit chewy breakfast treat, then you're welcome! The best thing about this recipe is the versatility of the toppings. Here I showcase a peanut butter and jelly overnight oatmeal using my 15-Minute Strawberry Chia Seed Jam from page 133. Feel free to experiment though! I love topping mine with applesauce, chocolate chips, sliced almonds, marmalade . . .

½ cup (45 g) rolled oats

½ cup (120 ml) oat milk

1 tbsp (15 ml) maple syrup

3 tbsp (48 g) peanut butter

¼ tsp salt

3 tbsp (45 g) 15-Minute Strawberry Chia Seed Jam (page 133) or your favorite jam

Fill the bottom of an 8-oz (237-ml) Mason jar with the oats and pour in the oat milk. Stir in the maple syrup, peanut butter and salt.

Put the lid on the Mason jar and store in the refrigerator overnight.

In the morning, gently stir the oats and heat in the microwave 30 seconds at a time until warmed. Add the jam and enjoy!

RECIPE NOTE

The oat milk I use for my 2-Step Overnight Oats is quite sweet. I add a tablespoon (15 ml) of maple syrup and use unsweetened peanut butter for the perfect-for-me sweetness. You may need to play with the amount of maple syrup depending on your personal sweet tooth.

Grab & Go Banana Bread **MUFFIN TOPS**

MAKES
8-10 MUFFIN TOPS

Ah . . . muffin tops . . . "where the muffin breaks free of the pan and does its own thing." At least according to Elaine Benes. And no—if you're a *Seinfeld* purist—I don't think you need to make muffin tops by discarding the "stumps." Food waste is a very un-vegan thing to do, after all. What I love most about this recipe (aside from how simple it is) is that it creates the perfect sized–breakfast. Great for a grab-and-go morning! And no worries if you don't have a muffin top pan. You can also make six to eight regular muffins with this recipe.

3 ripe bananas

1½ cups (188 g) all-purpose flour

½ cup (120 ml) maple syrup

¼ cup (56 g) coconut oil + more for brushing on the baking tin

1½ tsp (7 g) baking powder

¼ tsp salt

1 (3-oz [85-g]) vegan dark chocolate bar, cut into small chunks (see Recipe Note)

Preheat the oven to 350°F (175°C).

Peel the bananas and thoroughly mash them with a potato masher.

Combine the flour, maple syrup, ¼ cup (56 g) of coconut oil, baking powder and salt with the mashed banana. Mix well. Stir the chocolate chunks into the batter.

Lightly brush the muffin top baking pan with coconut oil. Fill each compartment with the batter. You want the batter to be just below the top edge of the muffin compartment.

Bake on the middle rack for about 20 minutes, until the tops are golden brown. Check the muffin tops by pricking with a toothpick. If the toothpick comes out clean, they are done. Allow to cool before storing in an airtight container.

RECIPE NOTE

When looking for vegan chocolate, don't be deterred by the inclusion of "cocoa butter" on the ingredient list. Cocoa butter is the oil-based fat found in the cocoa bean and is a dairy-free ingredient.

Simple & Sweet **GRANOLA**

A simple breakfast never tasted so good. This sweet and crunchy homemade granola is super easy to make and even easier to pack full of healthy vegan ingredients. It comes together in about 20 minutes and stores well, allowing you to have a hearty breakfast option throughout the week.

4 cups (360 g) rolled oats

1 tsp salt

⅓ cup (75 g) coconut oil

⅔ cup (160 ml) maple syrup

1 tsp vanilla extract

½ cup (69 g) pepitas

3 tbsp (21 g) flaxseed meal

Preheat the oven to 350°F (175°C).

In a large bowl, combine the oats, salt, coconut oil, maple syrup, vanilla extract, pepitas and flaxseed meal. Stir until thoroughly combined.

Evenly spread the granola mixture out on a baking sheet and bake for 20 minutes, stirring halfway. When the granola is golden brown, remove it from the oven and allow to cool completely. It will still be soft when it comes out of the oven but will become crispy as it cools.

RECIPE NOTE

Looking for a plant-based milk to enjoy with this granola? I recommend oat milk. It's creamy and doesn't have an overpowering flavor like many plant-based milks.

Basic Blueberry **BREAKFAST COOKIES**

With kids, breakfast often goes over better when it sounds like dessert. These breakfast cookies are made with just a few simple ingredients and are a winner every time. I make small batches of them when there's a banana on my counter that's threatening to stink up the joint. Such a good way to avoid food waste and send the kids off to school with healthy food in their systems.

1 ripe banana

2 cups (180 g) rolled oats

¼ cup (60 ml) maple syrup

½ cup (129 g) almond butter

1 tsp salt

½ cup (74 g) blueberries

Preheat the oven to 350°F (175°C). Prepare your baking sheet with parchment paper or a silicone baking mat.

In a large bowl, mash the banana using a potato masher until it resembles a paste.

Add the oats, maple syrup, almond butter, salt and blueberries. Stir to combine. The dough will have a loose consistency.

Using a large spoon, scoop a lime-sized ball of the dough onto the baking sheet. Gently flatten the dough to about 1 inch (2.5 cm) thick. Bake for 20 to 25 minutes.

The cookies will still be soft when they come out of the oven. Cool completely and store in an airtight container, separating each layer of cookies with parchment paper.

RECIPE NOTE

Because of the lack of preservatives, these breakfast cookies will become softer the longer they're contained. To get the most mileage out of your efforts, I recommend freezing the batter in premade cookie dough balls. That way, you can bake individual cookies in the morning as you need them.

SERVES
2

Presto! Pumpkin Pie **SMOOTHIES**

I love having smoothies in the morning. They're a quick, healthy breakfast. This autumn-inspired smoothie makes for a nice transition into cooler weather when making smoothies seems to fall by the wayside. Pumpkin pie spice is readily available in the spice aisle at the grocery store, and pumpkin puree is usually located with other canned fruit.

1 cup (240 ml) oat milk

½ cup (120 g) pumpkin puree

2 frozen bananas

1–2 dates, pitted (see Recipe Note)

1 tsp pumpkin pie spice

In a high-speed blender, combine the oat milk, pumpkin puree, bananas, dates and pumpkin pie spice. Blend until creamy.

RECIPE NOTE

Dates are nature's candy. They are very sweet! I find I only need one, but I don't have a big sweet tooth, so you might find that you want two. Dates can challenge even the highest-end blenders, so if your machine seems to be struggling, try soaking the dates in hot water for 10 minutes before blending.

SERVES

1

Super-Easy Superfood **SMOOTHIE**

This simple smoothie is a great way to get both fruits and veggies first thing in the morning. The frozen banana makes for a creamy consistency, and the date is a simple, unrefined way to add a little sweetness. You might also notice I have spinach on the list of ingredients. This often draws puzzled looks from smoothie newbies. Don't let it deter you though. The flavor of the bananas and blueberries makes the taste of spinach almost negligible.

1 cup (240 ml) oat milk

1 cup (30 g) baby spinach, loosely packed

1 cup (148 g) frozen blueberries

1 frozen banana

1 date, pitted (see Recipe Note)

In a high-speed blender, combine the oat milk, spinach, blueberries, banana and date. Blend until creamy.

RECIPE NOTE

Dates are nature's candy. They are very sweet! I find I only need one, but I don't have a big sweet tooth, so you might find that you want two. Dates can challenge even the highest-end blenders, so if your machine seems to be struggling, try soaking the dates in hot water for 10 minutes before blending.

NO SWEAT
SUNDAY
BRUNCH

More than having dinner with friends, I love gathering for Sunday brunch. There's just something about an idle midmorning meal. What I don't love is the food coma that often comes on afterward. Traditional brunch food tends to be luxurious and heavy . . . and accompanied by a mimosa or two. In this chapter, I wanted to capture all the upsides and none of the downsides of brunch. The following recipes are designed to be savory and comforting, but also light enough to keep that spring in your step for the rest of the day.

MAKES
8-10 WAFFLES

15-Minute Orange-Scented **WAFFLES**

Want to dazzle your family and friends by slaving over a hot stove to prepare the ultimate vegan Sunday brunch? This recipe will get you halfway there—as in, it has the dazzling part covered. As for slaving over a hot stove, I'm sure you've got much better plans for the weekend. This recipe is a twist on traditional vegan waffles, using orange juice instead of a plant-based milk. Top this iconic crispy-on-the-outside, fluffy-on-the-inside breakfast food with maple syrup and a sprinkle of orange zest, or really show it off by pairing it with my Easy Blueberry Compote (page 130).

1 tbsp (7 g) flaxseed meal

2 cups (250 g) all-purpose flour

2 tsp (9 g) baking powder

Pinch of salt

1¾ cups (420 ml) pulp-free orange juice

1 tbsp (14 g) coconut oil

2 tbsp (30 ml) maple syrup + more for topping

Fresh orange zest, for garnish (optional)

In a small bowl, mix the flaxseed meal and 3 tablespoons (45 ml) of water. It will become gelatinous. This is often called a flaxseed egg. Allow to rest for 5 minutes.

Preheat a waffle iron.

In a large bowl, add the flour, baking powder and salt. Stir to combine. In a separate bowl, combine the flaxseed egg, orange juice, coconut oil and maple syrup.

Add the wet ingredients to the dry ingredients and mix until the batter is smooth. Add the batter to the waffle iron and cook until golden brown, about 6 minutes.

Serve with fresh orange zest, if desired, and maple syrup.

Less Mess Baked Breakfast **LATKES**

MAKES
8-10 LATKES

Latkes used to be my nemesis. Every time I made them I swore I'd never make them again—all the spatter and used oil to discard! But with my other half being Jewish, I kept at it so that when Hanukkah came around we could honor some of his traditions. This vegan version of latkes is spatter-free and uses far less oil than traditional latkes, and the use of frozen hash browns makes it so easy! It replaces eggs with flaxseed meal, giving them a healthy boost as well. Many people like to eat their latkes with sour cream or applesauce, but I'm a fan of topping them with my Creamy Dill Dressing (page 146).

1 lb (454 g) pre-shredded frozen hash browns, defrosted overnight in the refrigerator

1 tsp salt

3 tbsp (21 g) flaxseed meal

½ cup (80 g) finely diced yellow onion

1 tbsp (9 g) minced garlic (see Recipe Notes)

4 tbsp (60 ml) safflower oil, divided + more for brushing latkes

⅛ tsp fresh ground pepper

2–4 chives, finely diced

Spread the defrosted hash browns evenly on a clean kitchen towel and sprinkle with the salt. Rest for 15 to 20 minutes. The salt will draw moisture from the potatoes.

In a small bowl, combine the flaxseed meal and ½ cup (120 ml) of water. Stir until thoroughly mixed. Allow to rest for 5 minutes. The flaxseed should become gelatinous. This combination is commonly called a flaxseed egg.

Preheat the oven to 350°F (175°C).

Pat the hash browns dry with a second clean kitchen towel. You want the potatoes to be as dry as possible.

Combine the hash browns, flaxseed egg, onion, garlic, 2 tablespoons (30 ml) of the safflower oil and the pepper. Mix well.

Using a basting brush, lightly spread ½ to 1 tablespoon (8 to 15 ml) of safflower oil onto a baking sheet. Shape the potato batter into thin cakes about 3 inches (7.5 cm) in diameter and ½ inch (1.3 cm) thick. Lightly brush the remaining safflower oil across the top of each latke. Bake for 40 minutes, flipping the latkes halfway through.

Increase the oven temperature to 425°F (220°C) and continue to bake the latkes for 10 minutes, until crispy. Serve immediately with the chives.

RECIPE NOTES

The latkes will be fragile on the first flip, but the flaxseed egg will continue to bind the ingredients as the latkes bake.

Two large cloves of garlic are about equal to 1 tablespoon (9 g) of minced garlic.

Scrambled Veggie **BREAKFAST HASH**

SERVES

4

Sunday morning breakfast hash used to be my go-to restaurant order. Of course, it used to include over-easy eggs, hash browns and plenty of cheddar cheese. Talk about sleep inducing. Not anymore. This much healthier version drops the eggs and hash browns and replaces them with creamy white beans. Slowly sautéed peppers, onions and garlic serve as the backdrop for a truly savory breakfast that will give you plenty of energy to enjoy the tail end of your weekend.

2 tbsp (30 ml) extra-virgin olive oil, divided

½ cup (80 g) yellow onion, diced, divided

1 tsp salt, divided

2 tbsp (18 g) minced garlic, divided (see Recipe Note)

2 tbsp (32 g) tomato paste

3 bell peppers, deseeded and diced

1 tbsp (6 g) cumin

1 (14-oz [397-g]) can cannellini beans, drained and rinsed

1 pint (300 g) fresh grape tomatoes, sliced (consider using multi-colored tomatoes)

Fresh cilantro, washed and torn (optional)

Fresh ground pepper, to taste

Add 1 tablespoon (15 ml) of the olive oil to a cast-iron skillet. Turn the burner to medium and heat until shimmering. Add half of the onion and ½ teaspoon of the salt. Reduce the heat to medium-low. Sauté the onion for 12 to 15 minutes, stirring occasionally, until golden brown.

While the onion is cooking, add the remaining olive oil to a small saucepan. When shimmering, add the remaining onion and ½ teaspoon of the salt and sauté on medium-low for 12 to 15 minutes, stirring occasionally, until golden brown.

Add 1 tablespoon (9 g) of the garlic to each pan. Sauté for 1 to 2 minutes.

Add the tomato paste to the cast-iron skillet and increase the heat to medium. Sauté the tomato paste until it becomes a deep, rich red, 2 to 3 minutes. Add the bell peppers and continue to sauté until they become soft, about 5 minutes. Set aside.

Add the cumin to the saucepan and sauté until fragrant, 1 to 2 minutes. Add the beans and 1 cup (240 ml) of water. Simmer for 15 minutes or until the beans are soft and easily mashed with a fork.

Add the tomatoes to the pepper hash and top with two large spoonfuls of mashed white beans. Serve with fresh cilantro, if using, and fresh ground pepper. For fun, you can give the white beans the appearance of eggs by placing half of a yellow grape tomato in the center.

RECIPE NOTE

Two large cloves of garlic are about equal to 1 tablespoon (9 g) of minced garlic.

SERVES
2

5-Ingredient **FRENCH TOAST**

I love the ingredients in this simple recipe. Instead of cream, butter and eggs, I use oat milk and flaxseed meal to create the thick custard that becomes the toast's exterior. Rather than frying the toast slices in a pan of butter, I like to bake them. It creates less mess and makes this already superior version of French toast even healthier. A tablespoon (15 ml) of maple syrup and a touch of vanilla extract add just the right amount of sweetness to this breakfast treat.

1½ cups (360 ml) oat milk

¼ cup (28 g) flaxseed meal

1 tbsp (15 ml) maple syrup + more for topping

1 tsp vanilla extract

8 slices of thick white bread, about 1½ inches (4 cm) thick (see Recipe Notes)

Powdered sugar, for topping (optional)

Preheat the oven to 400°F (205°C). Prepare a baking sheet with parchment paper or a silicone baking mat.

Combine the oat milk, flaxseed meal, maple syrup and vanilla extract in a pie tin. Set aside for 10 minutes to allow the flaxseed meal to absorb the milk. This creates the "custard."

Dip both sides of each bread slice into the oat milk mixture and place it on the baking sheet.

Bake for 30 minutes, flipping each piece halfway through. The French toast should be golden brown and crispy on the outside when finished.

Serve immediately with warmed maple syrup and powdered sugar, if desired.

RECIPE NOTES

Planning a special brunch? Try topping this French toast with my Vegan Caramel Sauce (page 120).

I don't recommend using traditional sandwich bread for this recipe. It is difficult to get the crispy-on-the-outside, soft-on-the-inside result. Challah and brioche are lovely but are rarely vegan. I chose a thick French bread loaf for this recipe and it worked beautifully.

Spinach & Tomato MINI QUICHES

MAKES
6-8 MINI QUICHES

If you've looked into vegan brunch ideas, you probably know that many vegan quiche recipes call for tofu as their base. I get it. When used in a vegan quiche recipe, tofu takes on a texture similar to cooked eggs. Try as I might, though, I just can't do tofu for breakfast. This recipe, which uses a combination of cashew cream and chickpea flour to create the filling, hits the spot. I fill it with plenty of sautéed tomatoes and spinach as well as some nutritional yeast—which has a nice, cheesy flavor—for an easy, healthy brunch option.

1 cup (146 g) cashews

1 tbsp (15 ml) safflower oil + additional for greasing the muffin tin

½ tsp salt

½ cup (80 g) finely diced yellow onion

1 tbsp (9 g) minced garlic (see Recipe Note)

1 cup (155 g) grape tomatoes, sliced, setting aside about 16 slices to top the quiches

3 cups (90 g) baby spinach, roughly torn, setting aside about 16 leaves to top the quiches

2 tbsp (10 g) nutritional yeast

1 tbsp (15 ml) lemon juice

1 cup (92 g) chickpea flour

Fresh ground pepper, to taste

In a glass measuring cup, combine the cashews with 2 cups (480 ml) of just-boiling water. Set aside for 30 minutes.

Preheat the oven to 400°F (205°C).

While the cashews are soaking, add a tablespoon (15 ml) of safflower oil to a small skillet. Turn the burner to medium and heat until shimmering. Reduce the heat to medium-low and add the salt and onion. Sauté the onion until golden brown, 12 to 15 minutes. Add the garlic and continue sautéing for 1 to 2 minutes. Add the sliced tomatoes and spinach. Sauté until the spinach is wilted. Set aside.

Drain and rinse the cashews. In a high-speed blender, combine the cashews with ¾ cup (180 ml) of water, the nutritional yeast and lemon juice. Blend until creamy.

In a large bowl, combine the cashew cream with the chickpea flour and ½ cup (120 ml) of water. Stir until well combined. Add the cooked onion, garlic, tomatoes and spinach.

Lightly grease a muffin tin with safflower oil and pour the batter into each compartment. Top each mini quiche with ground pepper, spinach leaves and sliced tomatoes. Bake for 12 to 15 minutes. Check the quiches by pricking with a toothpick. If the toothpick comes out clean, the quiches are done.

RECIPE NOTE
Two large cloves of garlic are about equal to 1 tablespoon (9 g) of minced garlic.

MAKES
2 SLICES (WITH
PICKLED RED
ONIONS TO SPARE)

AVOCADO TOAST with Pickled Red Onions

This simple combination is one of my favorite brunch recipes (am I allowed to pick favorites?). Seriously though, pickled red onions are my unicorn food. They're super easy to make and keep in the refrigerator for weeks. The combination of the avocado's creaminess and the tartness of the pickled red onions wakes my taste buds right up. And that color combination? That's what avocado toast dreams are made of.

1 cup (240 ml) rice wine vinegar (see Recipe Notes)

1 tbsp (15 g) sugar

1 tsp salt

1 large red onion, peeled and thinly sliced

2 slices sourdough bread

1 avocado

Salt and fresh ground pepper, to taste

Toasted Pumpkin Seeds (page 142; optional)

In a medium-sized saucepan, bring the rice wine vinegar and 1 cup (240 ml) of water to a boil. Add the sugar and salt and stir until dissolved. Allow to cool.

Tightly pack the sliced onion into a 12-oz (340-g) Mason jar and carefully pour the cooled vinegar solution into the jar. Refrigerate overnight.

Toast two slices of sourdough bread. While the bread is toasting, thinly slice the avocado.

Spread the avocado slices on the toast and top with the pickled red onions. Season with salt and fresh ground pepper to taste. Sprinkle on some Toasted Pumpkin Seeds, if using.

RECIPE NOTES

You can experiment with different vinegars when pickling onions. I like rice wine vinegar the best. It's not quite as pucker-inducing as apple cider or white wine vinegar.

Wondering what to do with leftover pickled red onions? Add them to my Basic Breakfast Burrito Bowls (page 91) to make a killer breakfast, or top my Easy Jackfruit Taquitos (page 113) with them for some extra kick!

15-Minute Apple Cinnamon **MINI PANCAKES**

These easy apple cinnamon mini pancakes are a great way to add a little flair to ordinary pancakes—especially when the weather starts to cool and autumn is in the air. The sweet smell of cinnamon will draw even the sleepiest family members out of bed. I like to serve these fresh off the griddle with apple slices and warmed maple syrup.

2 cups (250 g) all-purpose flour

2 tsp (9 g) baking powder

Pinch of salt

½ cup (120 ml) unsweetened applesauce

1 tbsp (14 g) coconut oil

2 tbsp (30 ml) maple syrup + more for drizzling on pancakes

½ tsp cinnamon

Apple slices, for garnish (optional)

Preheat your griddle.

In a large bowl, mix the flour, baking powder and salt. Stir to combine.

In a separate bowl, combine 1½ cups (360 ml) of water, the applesauce, coconut oil, maple syrup and cinnamon.

Add the wet ingredients to the dry ingredients and mix until the batter is smooth. If the batter is too thick, add additional water 1 tablespoon (15 ml) at a time.

Pour the batter onto your griddle to make 3- to 4-inch (8- to 10-cm) pancakes. When air bubbles begin to appear on the top of the pancakes, inspect the bottom for a golden-brown color before flipping. This should take 2 to 3 minutes. Flip the pancakes and cook the other side for 2 to 3 minutes. Serve with apple slices, if desired, and maple syrup.

SERVES

4

Basic Breakfast **BURRITO BOWLS**

Red lentil breakfast burritos were my go-to recipe when I first started cooking vegan at home. Well, sort of. I started out by mixing red lentils in with my scrambled eggs and cheese. Then I gradually stopped using the eggs, followed by the cheese. These ingredients were replaced with healthier options like avocado and spinach. Some days I'll still wrap these ingredients up in a tortilla, but most of the time I like to let the lentils do the talking and just serve them up in a bowl with my favorite hot sauce.

1 tbsp (15 ml) extra-virgin olive oil

1 cup (160 g) yellow onion, finely chopped

1 tbsp (9 g) minced garlic (see Recipe Note)

1 tbsp (6 g) cumin

2 tbsp (32 g) tomato paste

1 cup (192 g) red lentils, rinsed and picked clean of debris

1 pint (300 g) grape tomatoes, diced

1 avocado, thinly sliced

Cilantro, washed and torn (optional)

Tortillas, toasted and seasoned with olive oil and a sprinkle of chili powder (optional)

Add the olive oil to a large, deep-sided skillet. Turn the burner to medium and heat until shimmering. Add the onion and reduce the heat to medium-low. Sauté the onion until it is golden brown, 12 to 15 minutes. Add the garlic and sauté for 1 to 2 minutes. Add the cumin and continue cooking until fragrant, about 1 minute.

Increase the heat to medium and add the tomato paste. Sauté until it becomes dark red in color, 2 to 3 minutes. Add the lentils and stir to coat. Add 2 cups (480 ml) of water and bring the lentils to a simmer.

Simmer, covered, for 20 minutes, stirring occasionally. Add more water ½ cup (120 ml) at a time if necessary. When finished, the lentils should be soft. Gently mash the lentils.

Serve immediately, topped with the tomatoes, sliced avocado and cilantro, if using. Serve with the tortillas, if desired. If you have any leftover pickled red onions from my avocado toast recipe (page 87) think about adding those too!

RECIPE NOTE

Two large cloves of garlic are about equal to 1 tablespoon (9 g) of minced garlic.

Easy Vegan "CHORIZO"

I know, I know. This recipe is kind of ugly. Sausage—even vegan sausage—just does not have a good side. What it lacks in visual aesthetics, though, it makes up for in taste. Packed with healthy beans and nuts, it's one of my favorites dishes to take on my family's summer camping trips. It's spicy and savory and only uses a few easy-to-find ingredients! Pack it in your breakfast burritos or serve it alongside my Spinach & Tomato Mini Quiches (page 84).

1 cup (117 g) walnuts

1 (8-oz [227-g]) jar sun-dried tomatoes, packed in oil

½ cup (80 g) roughly chopped yellow onion

1 tbsp (9 g) roughly chopped garlic (see Recipe Notes)

1 (25-oz [709-g]) can kidney beans, drained and rinsed

1 tbsp (7 g) chorizo seasoning (see Recipe Notes)

Extra-virgin olive oil, for basting

Salt and pepper, to taste

Preheat the oven to 400°F (205°C).

Evenly spread the walnuts out on a baking sheet. Toast in the oven for 10 minutes, checking periodically after 5 minutes to avoid burning. Set aside.

Reduce the oven temperature to 350°F (175°C).

Drain the tomatoes, reserving the oil. You should have approximately ½ cup (120 ml) of reserved oil. If you do not have ½ cup (120 ml) of the oil, you can supplement with extra-virgin olive oil. Roughly chop the tomatoes.

In a food processor, combine the tomatoes, onion, garlic, walnuts and the reserved oil. Pulse until the walnuts and tomatoes are reduced to small pieces. Add the kidney beans and the chorizo seasoning and pulse until the beans have a cooked oatmeal-like consistency. The mixture will be wet.

Using a basting brush, lightly coat a baking sheet with olive oil. Evenly spread the bean mixture onto the baking sheet. Bake on the middle rack for 20 minutes.

Stir the mixture. It should be beginning to dry. Continue baking for 10 minutes, then stir. Bake for another 10 minutes. The chorizo should be crumbly—but not crunchy—when done. Season with salt and pepper, to taste.

RECIPE NOTES

Two large cloves of garlic are about equal to 1 tablespoon (9 g) of minced garlic.

Chorizo seasoning can usually be found in the ethnic food section at your grocery store or online at a specialty spice shop, like savoryspiceshop.com. Still can't find chorizo seasoning? You can substitute taco seasoning. It works very well in a pinch!

SERVES
1

Golden Milk **LATTE**

I once made these and brought them on a February yurt trip with some girlfriends. They made for a delightful post-ski treat! What's a yurt, you ask? Why it's a round canvas tent. Now you know why we needed hot lattes! Whether I'm winter sporting in the great outdoors or snuggled on the couch with a book, I do love having a Golden Milk Latte by my side. The turmeric/pepper combination is good for your health and for your soul. It's warm and sweet and oh. so. cozy.

1 cup (240 ml) oat milk

1 tsp coconut oil (optional; see Recipe Note)

1 tbsp (15 ml) maple syrup

1 tsp turmeric

¼ tsp ginger powder

¼ tsp cinnamon

Pinch of black pepper (optional; see Recipe Note)

In a small saucepan, bring the oat milk to a low simmer. When simmering, add the coconut oil, if using, maple syrup, turmeric, ginger powder, cinnamon and black pepper, if using. Stir and simmer on low for 1 to 2 minutes. Remove from the heat and enjoy.

RECIPE NOTE
Coconut oil and black pepper help your body to process turmeric.

MINIMAL-INGREDIENT MUNCHIES
and
PRE-DINNER DELIGHTS

Who doesn't love apps? In this chapter, I wanted to honor my own personal view of appetizers: they exist purely for enjoyment. By their very definition, appetizers are intended to tease the taste buds and stimulate the appetite. In the traditional sense, that usually means creamy and cheesy and deep fried (I'm looking at you, fried mozzarella sticks). This might prompt you to think, "Alas, this is a vegan cookbook. These apps won't be any fun." You'd be wrong though. These appetizers are every bit as enticing as their fast-casual restaurant chain counterparts.

SMASHED POTATOES with French Onion Dip

SERVES
4

Forget sour cream and onion potato chips. This recipe takes that tired game day snack and gives it new life. Smashing your potatoes creates much more surface area for creating a crispy exterior. And while dairy-free French onion dip sounds like an impossibility, substituting sour cream with creamy cashews makes for an amazing sauce.

1 cup (146 g) cashews

2 tbsp (28 g) vegan butter (see Recipe Note)

2 yellow onions, peeled and thinly sliced

1½ lbs (681 g) fingerling potatoes, washed

2 tbsp (30 ml) safflower oil, divided

1 tsp salt

1 clove garlic

2 tbsp (10 g) nutritional yeast

1 tbsp (15 ml) fresh lemon juice

1 tbsp (4 g) parsley, washed, destemmed and roughly chopped

Fresh ground pepper, to taste

Soak the cashews in 2 cups (480 ml) of just-boiling water. Set aside for 30 minutes.

Add the butter to a medium-sized skillet. Turn the burner to medium and heat until the butter is melted. Reduce the heat to its lowest setting and add the onions, crowding them in the pan. Slowly cook the onions until they start to release their moisture, about 10 minutes, then cover the skillet.

Allow the onions to cook with the cover on for about 20 minutes, stirring every 5 minutes. After 20 minutes, remove the cover and continue to cook until they are deeply browned, about 1 hour. Stir every 5 minutes. Be careful not to burn the onions, especially as they near completion.

While the onions are caramelizing, add 1 to 2 inches (2.5 to 5 cm) of water to a large stockpot and fit with a steamer basket. Bring the water to a boil. Add the potatoes and steam until they are easily pierced with a fork, 20 to 25 minutes.

Preheat the oven to 400°F (205°C).

Remove the steamed potatoes from the steamer basket. Grease a large baking sheet with a tablespoon (15 ml) of the safflower oil. Arrange the potatoes on the baking sheet, keeping space between each potato. Using a potato masher, smash each of the potatoes. Baste with the remaining tablespoon (15 ml) of safflower oil and sprinkle with the salt. Roast until crispy and golden, about 15 to 20 minutes.

When the onions are almost done cooking, drain and rinse the cashews. In a high-speed blender, add the cashews, ¾ cup (180 ml) of water, garlic, nutritional yeast and lemon juice. Blend until creamy. Remove the sauce from the blender and stir in the caramelized onions.

Spoon the onion dip onto the smashed potatoes. Top with the parsley and fresh ground pepper.

RECIPE NOTE

The type of vegan butter used in this recipe matters. Oil-based vegan butters and buttery spreads won't brown. Instead choose a nut-based butter. The proteins will react with the sugars when heat is applied, leading to browning.

DELICATA SQUASH FRIES
with Lemon-Garlic Aioli

Move over potatoes, there's a new fry in town! These delicata squash fries are a tasty twist on one of America's food darlings. Baking the squash instead of frying makes it much healthier. Salting the squash before roasting it draws out the moisture, allowing the fries to crisp up in the oven. These squash fries are wonderful on their own—especially if you add plenty of pepper (yes, I am a pepper-your-fries person)—but they're especially good paired with lemon-garlic aioli.

SERVES
2

2 delicata squash

2 tsp (12 g) salt

1 tbsp (15 ml) safflower oil

¼ tsp pepper

¼ cup (60 ml) vegan mayonnaise

1 tbsp (15 ml) fresh lemon juice

1 small clove garlic, finely minced

1 tsp lemon zest (optional)

Preheat the oven to 425°F (220°C).

Thoroughly wash each squash and trim the ends. There is no need to peel the squash. Place each squash on a trimmed end and carefully slice in half lengthwise. Scoop out the seeds.

Using a sharp knife, slice each half of the squash into thirds (widthwise) and then into thin "fries" about ½ inch (1.3 cm) thick.

Lay the squash fries out on a clean kitchen towel and sprinkle with the salt. Rest for 15 minutes. The squash will shed moisture, helping the fries to become crispy in the oven.

Pat the fries dry and toss them in the safflower oil. Lay the fries out evenly on a large baking sheet. Sprinkle with the pepper. Roast the fries on the middle rack, cut side down, for 25 minutes. Flip the fries and cook for 20 more minutes. Carefully watch the fries in the second half of roasting. Turn the baking sheet as necessary to avoid burning.

While the fries are roasting, prepare the aioli by combining the mayonnaise, lemon juice and garlic. Garnish with lemon zest, if desired.

Serve the squash fries immediately with the lemon-garlic aioli on the side.

RECIPE NOTE
Like their Idaho potato counterparts, delicata squash fries don't reheat well. These are best served right out of the oven. Don't worry though, you won't have leftovers.

Homemade **PRETZEL BITES**

Vegans and lazy football Sundays just got a little cozier. Soft pretzels are a great snack for people to gather around. When you make them from scratch, you'll get that perfect soft-on-the-inside, chewy-on-the-outside texture. Make the effort to find a coarse grain sea salt for the top. Getting that little nugget of salt in each bite really makes a soft pretzel. I like to pair mine with Dijon mustard and pizza sauce. If you want to up your pre-game though, be sure to serve them with a side of my Chipotle Ranch Dressing. You can find the recipe on page 145.

1 (0.25-oz [7-g]) package active dry yeast

1 tbsp (15 ml) maple syrup

1 tbsp (15 ml) extra-virgin olive oil + more for greasing bowl

2½ cups (313 g) all-purpose flour

1 tsp salt

2 tbsp (28 g) baking soda

Coarse-ground flaky sea salt

Mix the yeast in 1 cup (240 ml) of very hot water (about 110°F [43°C]). Stir in the maple syrup and olive oil. Set aside and allow the yeast to activate, about 5 minutes. The yeast should bubble and form a foam on the water's surface.

In a large bowl, combine the flour and salt. Combine the wet and dry ingredients and mix well. Knead the dough until smooth. Set aside in a lightly oiled bowl and cover with a slightly damp towel. Allow the dough to rise for 30 minutes.

Preheat the oven to 400°F (205°C). Prepare a baking sheet with a layer of parchment paper.

After the dough has risen, knead it three to four times and roll it into two 18-inch (45-cm) ropes about 2 inches (5 cm) in diameter. Cut each rope into 1-inch (2.5-cm) pieces. Set each piece on to the parchment paper, covering the cut dough with a slightly dampened kitchen towel as you work.

Prepare the alkaline bath—this is what makes the pretzels chewy—by bringing 6 cups (1.4 L) of water and the baking soda to a boil.

Working in small batches, drop the pretzel bites into the alkaline bath for approximately 30 seconds and then place them on the baking sheet. Sprinkle with the coarse sea salt.

Bake the pretzels on the middle rack for 15 minutes—keeping an eye on the bites as they bake—until they are golden brown.

RECIPE NOTE

To reheat these pretzels, wrap them in a slightly damp paper towel and microwave for 20 seconds. This will keep them from drying out and becoming stale.

Roasted Garlic, White Bean and Broccolini
FLATBREAD

SERVES
2

This vegan-friendly appetizer has so many wonderful flavors happening at once. Perhaps my favorite is the peppery roasted broccolini. The creamy, white bean garlic spread is a close second. For this recipe, I took the extra step of making my own crust. It's simple, stays within the five ingredients and makes this flatbread taste even better.

1 head garlic

⅓ cup (80 ml) + 3 tbsp (45 ml) extra-virgin olive oil, divided

2 bunches broccolini, washed and cut into large florets

1½ tsp (9 g) salt, divided

⅛ tsp pepper + more for topping

1 (0.25-oz [7-g]) package active dry yeast

1 tbsp (15 ml) maple syrup

2½ cups (313 g) all-purpose flour + more for work surface and pizza stone

1 (14-oz [397-g]) can cannellini beans, drained and rinsed

2 tbsp (30 ml) fresh lemon juice

Lemon zest, to taste

Preheat the oven to 400°F (205°C).

Cut the top quarter off the head of garlic, exposing the cloves. Place the garlic, cut side up, in aluminum foil and drizzle with 1 tablespoon (15 ml) of olive oil. Wrap up the foil and roast for 1 hour.

When the garlic has roasted for 40 minutes, toss the broccolini in 1 tablespoon (15 ml) of olive oil and season with ½ teaspoon of the salt and the pepper. Roast on the middle rack until the broccolini is slightly charred, 20 to 25 minutes.

While the garlic and broccolini are roasting, make the flatbread dough. Combine the yeast with 1 cup (240 ml) of hot water (about 110°F [43°C]). Add 1 tablespoon (15 ml) of the olive oil and maple syrup. Stir to combine and allow to rest for 5 minutes. The yeast should activate, creating bubbles and a foam on the water's surface.

Combine the 2½ cups (313 g) of flour and 1 teaspoon of salt in a large mixing bowl. Add the yeast mixture and stir to form the dough. It should be firm and not sticky to the touch. If it is too sticky, add more flour 1 tablespoon (8 g) at a time. If it is too dry, add more water 1 tablespoon (15 ml) at a time.

Lightly flour a dry surface and knead the dough for 1 to 2 minutes to form a ball. Divide the ball in half and roll one section out to make the flatbread crust. You can freeze the other half of the dough for later use.

When the garlic and broccolini have finished roasting, increase the oven temperature to 500°F (260°C) and preheat a pizza stone or pizza tray.

When the stone is hot, dust the surface with a light layer of flour and lay the rolled-out dough on to the stone. Pierce with a fork to prevent air bubbles. Bake for 10 minutes.

Combine the roasted garlic, cannellini beans, ⅓ cup (80 ml) of olive oil and lemon juice in a small food processor. Blend until creamy. Spread the roasted garlic and white bean mixture on the baked flatbread crust. Top with the roasted broccolini and return to the oven to bake until hot, about 5 minutes.

Serve immediately with fresh ground pepper and lemon zest.

MAKES
APPROXIMATELY
3 CUPS (738 G)

Creamy **HUMMUS**

Who doesn't love hummus? This recipe uses dried chickpeas instead of canned. Using dried chickpeas results in a creamier, less beany flavor, and the tahini gives this hummus that delightful tanginess. Much of hummus's appeal comes from getting creative with its toppings. I like toasted pine nuts, extra-virgin olive oil, sweet paprika, parsley and lemon zest on mine. Not only do these ingredients add flavor, they make this vegan appetizer visually appealing.

2 cups (400 g) dried chickpeas, soaked overnight (see Recipe Notes)

⅓ cup (45 g) pine nuts (see Recipe Notes)

½ cup (130 g) tahini

½ cup (120 ml) extra-virgin olive oil

½ cup (120 ml) fresh lemon juice

3 cloves garlic

1 tsp salt

¼ tsp pepper

½ cup (30 g) fresh parsley, washed, destemmed and torn

¼ tsp sweet paprika

Lemon zest, to taste

In a medium-sized saucepan, bring 4 cups (960 ml) of water and the soaked chickpeas to a boil. Simmer until the chickpeas are soft, about 1 hour. Drain and rinse.

While the chickpeas are simmering, gently toast the pine nuts in a dry skillet on medium heat until they are golden brown, 2 to 3 minutes.

In a food processor, combine the chickpeas, tahini, olive oil, lemon juice, garlic, salt and pepper. Combine until creamy, 3 to 5 minutes. If the hummus is too thick, add water 1 tablespoon (15 ml) at a time.

Top with the toasted pine nuts, parsley, paprika and lemon zest.

RECIPE NOTES

In a pinch, you can use canned chickpeas. Drain and rinse them first, then lay them out on a clean kitchen towel. Cover with a second clean towel and gently rub the chickpeas between the two towels to remove the skins. Simmer for 20 to 25 minutes until tender.

Pine nuts are delicate and high in fat. This gives them a creamy consistency that adds richness to this dish. Because of the fat content they do burn quickly, so be sure to keep an eye on them as they're toasting.

One-Dish Chickpea "TUNA" SALAD

SERVES
2

This vegan version of a tuna salad is a force to be reckoned with. The trick is to remove the skins from the chickpeas before you mix the salad. It makes for a much better texture. Red onion and pickle brine make this tuna salad stand-in every bit as good as the original. I like to pack it between two pieces of toasted classic sandwich bread, and if I feel the need, I will crunch up some potato chips and sprinkle them in. What can I say? Old habits die hard.

1 (14-oz [397-g]) can chickpeas, drained and rinsed

¼ cup (60 ml) vegan mayonnaise

2 tbsp (20 g) dill pickles, finely chopped + 1 tbsp (15 ml) dill pickle brine (see Recipe Note)

2 tbsp (20 g) finely diced red onion

2 tbsp (14 g) sliced almonds

Salt and fresh ground pepper, to taste

Drain and rinse the chickpeas with cold water. Lay them out on a clean kitchen towel. Lay another clean kitchen towel on top and gently rub the chickpeas between the two towels. This will loosen the skins. Continue this process until most of the skins have been removed. The more you can remove the better, but you do not need to remove them all.

Using a potato masher, gently mash the chickpeas. Leave some larger pieces intact. Add the mayonnaise, pickles, brine, red onion and sliced almonds. Stir to combine.

Refrigerate the salad for about 1 hour, until chilled, then season with salt and pepper.

RECIPE NOTE

Not all dill pickles are created equal. For this recipe, I like to use dill pickles that have a spicy, mustardy flavor. Look for a brine that includes mustard seeds and red pepper flakes.

EDAMAME DUMPLINGS
with Tamari Dipping Sauce

Want to dazzle your friends with an epic vegan appetizer? These edamame dumplings are a crowd-pleaser. Dumplings take a little extra time to fold, but the aesthetics are worth it. And just wait until your friends get a taste! The blended edamame gives the filling a creamy texture. The real showstopper, though, is the black truffle oil. If you haven't tried this before, trust me—it's a flavor that can't be recreated any other way. Make the effort to get a good, high-quality bottle and be sure to give it some prime real estate in your refrigerator to make it last.

1 (12-oz [340-g]) package of vegan wonton wrappers

1 (12-oz [340-g]) bag frozen, shelled edamame

2 tbsp (30 ml) + 1 tsp extra-virgin olive oil, divided

4 tbsp (60 ml) rice wine vinegar, divided

1 tbsp (15 ml) black truffle oil

1 tsp salt

2 tsp (10 g) sugar, divided

½ cup (120 ml) tamari sauce

2 scallions, thinly sliced, separating the white parts from the green parts

White and black sesame seeds, for garnish (optional)

Remove the wonton wrappers from the refrigerator and bring to room temperature. This will make them easier to fold.

Fill a small saucepan with a shallow amount of water, about 2 inches (5 cm). Bring to a boil and add the frozen edamame. Simmer until the edamame is bright green, 4 to 6 minutes. Drain and rinse.

In a food processor, combine the edamame, 2 tablespoons (30 ml) of olive oil, 2 tablespoons (30 ml) of rice wine vinegar, the truffle oil, salt and 1 teaspoon of sugar. Blend, leaving some larger pieces of edamame intact.

Prepare a baking sheet with parchment paper.

Place one wonton wrapper on a clean, dry surface. Brush the edges of the wrapper with water. Place about 1 tablespoon (16 g) of the edamame mixture into the center of the wrapper. Fold the wrapper in half and gently pinch the edges opposite of the fold into a pleated pattern. Lay the folded dumpling onto the baking sheet and cover with a slightly dampened kitchen towel. This will keep the dumplings from drying out. Continue until all of the edamame filling has been used. Carefully cover the baking sheet and store the dumplings in the refrigerator until you are ready to cook.

To prepare the dipping sauce, combine the tamari sauce, ½ cup (120 ml) of water and 2 tablespoons (30 ml) of the rice wine vinegar in a small saucepan. Bring to a boil. Add 1 teaspoon of the sugar and whisk until the sugar dissolves, about 1 minute. Set aside.

When ready to serve, place a steamer basket in a large stockpot with 1 to 2 inches (2.5 to 5 cm) of water. Lightly grease the steamer basket with a teaspoon of the olive oil then bring the water to a boil. Gently lay each dumpling in the steamer basket, making sure to keep the dumplings separate. Cover and steam for 4 minutes.

Serve with the tamari dipping sauce and top with the scallion greens and sesame seeds, if using.

MAKES
APPROXIMATELY
10 TAQUITOS

Easy Jackfruit **TAQUITOS**

Every time I make taquitos using this basic recipe I marvel at how satisfying they are. I used to think that deep frying was the only way to accomplish a crispy exterior, but this recipe has a simple trick using—drumroll please!—water. Yes, that's right: water. By simply soaking your corn tortillas in a pan of boiling water, you can achieve almost the same satisfying crunch as you can by deep frying. To make these finger foods even healthier, I substitute cheese with slices of avocado and use jackfruit spiced with taco seasoning as the main ingredient.

2 tbsp (30 ml) safflower oil + more for brushing on baking sheet

½ cup (80 g) yellow onion, diced

2 (20-oz [567-g]) cans young jackfruit

1 tbsp (9 g) minced garlic (see Recipe Note)

2 tbsp (12 g) taco seasoning

10 (6-inch [15-cm]) corn tortillas

1 cup (155 g) grape tomatoes, sliced

½ cup (69 g) Toasted Pumpkin Seeds (page 142)

Chipotle Ranch Dressing (page 145; optional)

Cilantro, torn (optional)

Preheat the oven to 425°F (220°C).

Add the safflower oil to a medium-sized skillet. Turn the burner to medium and heat until shimmering. Add the onion and reduce the heat to medium-low. Sauté the onion until golden brown, 12 to 15 minutes.

While the onion is cooking, drain and rinse the jackfruit. Using a sharp knife, cut the jackfruit into bite-size pieces. It will naturally shred as you do this. To further shred, use two forks and pull the remaining pieces of the jackfruit apart. Wrap the pulled jackfruit in a clean kitchen towel and squeeze to remove excess water.

Once the onion has cooked to golden brown, add the garlic and sauté for 1 to 2 minutes. Add the jackfruit and the taco seasoning. Increase the heat to medium-high and cook the jackfruit until it begins to crisp. Remove from the heat and set aside.

In a deep-sided skillet, bring 1 to 2 inches (2.5 to 5 cm) of water to a boil. While the water is coming to a boil, prepare a baking sheet by brushing it with a thin layer of safflower oil.

One by one, place each corn tortilla into the boiling water for 10 seconds. Using tongs, remove the tortilla and allow any excess water to drip back into the skillet. Lay the tortilla on the baking sheet and place about 2 tablespoons (32 g) of the jackfruit mixture in the bottom third of the tortilla. Starting from the bottom, roll the tortilla tightly and secure each end with a toothpick.

Bake the taquitos on the middle rack for 12 to 15 minutes until browned and crispy. Serve with sliced tomatoes and Toasted Pumpkin Seeds. For additional spice, try adding my Chipotle Ranch Dressing, if desired. Cilantro, if used, adds aesthetic appeal.

RECIPE NOTE
Two large cloves of garlic are about equal to 1 tablespoon (9 g) of minced garlic.

SIMPLY SERVING
the SWEET TOOTH

Ah—dessert! While I don't have a massive sweet tooth—I'll take French fries over chocolate cake any day—I do like a little something to punctuate the end of the day. What I've discovered since adopting a mostly plant-based diet is that dessert doesn't have to be all butter, flour and sugar. In fact, it's quite easy to create a dreamy dessert without these ingredients. In this chapter, I'll show you how vegan-friendly ingredients like chickpeas, dates, cashews and tofu (yes, tofu) can satisfy even the most die-hard dessert connoisseur.

Minimalist Chocolate-Espresso **MOUSSE**

SERVES
4

I'd like to use this opportunity to amend Otto von Bismarck's quote to "If you like laws and sausages [and vegan chocolate mousse], you should never watch ~~either one of~~ them being made." I will admit, I initially balked at the idea of making vegan chocolate mousse with tofu. It just seemed so undessert-like. And, fair warning, silken tofu has a . . . shall we say . . . off-putting texture right out of the box. What can I say? I'm not the kind of vegan cook that waxes poetic about tofu's visual appeal. But once you try this recipe, you'll be (like me) a total convert. I wouldn't have included it in this book unless I was convinced that the end result—a light and airy, slightly sweet, slightly bitter piece of dessert heaven—would be worth it.

1 tsp coconut oil

½ cup (84 g) semisweet dark vegan chocolate, roughly chopped (see Recipe Notes)

12 oz (340 g) silken tofu

1 tsp espresso extract

Coconut whipped cream (see Recipe Notes)

Fresh raspberries, washed

In a microwave-safe glass measuring cup, combine the coconut oil and chocolate pieces. Melt the chocolate in the microwave 30 seconds at a time, stirring between sessions, until completely melted.

In a high-speed blender, combine the melted chocolate, silken tofu and espresso extract. Blend until smooth.

Pour the mixture into individual serving containers and refrigerate for 1 hour. Serve with the coconut whipped cream and fresh raspberries.

RECIPE NOTES

I use semisweet dark vegan chocolate to make this dish. Between that and the coconut whipped cream, there is just the right amount of sweetness. If you find the mousse too bitter (you can taste it before chilling) you can add a small amount of maple syrup to sweeten it up.

When looking for vegan chocolate, don't be deterred by the inclusion of "cocoa butter" on the ingredient list. Cocoa butter is the oil-based fat found in the cocoa bean and is a dairy-free ingredient.

Coconut whipped cream can be found in the freezer section at the grocery store. Note that it often requires about 4 hours to defrost in the refrigerator before it can be served.

Chickpea Chocolate Chip **COOKIE DOUGH**

MAKES
APPROXIMATELY
3 CUPS (672 G)

And you thought silken tofu chocolate mousse was going to give you pause? (See the previous recipe.) Yes, cookie dough. Made with chickpeas. Cheer up though—you won't get salmonella poisoning eating this one raw by the spoonful. That's how it's intended to be consumed. Like my Creamy Hummus recipe (page 106), I highly recommend using dried chickpeas and soaking them overnight. They have a much less beany taste than the canned version. Combine them with some vanilla extract, maple syrup and peanut butter and you'll be amazed by how the taste and texture reminds you of your younger years when you ate Toll House® cookie dough directly from the tube.

1½ cups (300 g) dry chickpeas

½ cup (129 g) peanut butter

¼ cup (60 ml) maple syrup

1 tsp vanilla extract

½ cup (84 g) vegan semisweet chocolate chips (see Recipe Note)

Soak the chickpeas in 4 cups (960 ml) of water. Cover and allow to sit overnight.

Drain and rinse the chickpeas. Bring 4 cups (960 ml) of water to a simmer in a small saucepan. Simmer the chickpeas until soft, about 1 hour. Drain and rinse with cold water.

In a food processor, combine the cooked chickpeas, peanut butter, maple syrup and vanilla extract. Blend until smooth, then stir in the chocolate chips. Make sure that the "batter" is sufficiently cool before adding the chocolate.

Refrigerate for 1 hour before serving.

RECIPE NOTE

When looking for vegan chocolate, don't be deterred by the inclusion of "cocoa butter" on the ingredient list. Cocoa butter is the oil-based fat found in the cocoa bean and is a dairy-free ingredient.

Vegan CARAMEL SAUCE

MAKES
APPROXIMATELY
1 CUP (240 ML)

Did you know that traditional caramel sauce is made by browning sugar and combining it with heavy cream and butter? It's a magnet for a sweet tooth if ever there was one. For this recipe, I wanted to make a vegan version using a natural sweetener—dates! These soft, chewy delights are practically nature's version of caramel. I swapped out the heavy cream with homemade cashew cream—don't worry, it's easier than it sounds—reduced the amount of butter and replaced it with a vegan version. This vegan dessert topping is dreamy, and unlike its cream-based cousin, it won't get stuck in your teeth!

1 cup (146 g) cashews

8 medjool dates, pitted

1 tbsp (15 ml) maple syrup

2 tbsp (28 g) vegan butter

⅛ tsp salt

1 tsp vanilla extract

Soak the cashews in just-boiling water for 30 minutes.

Soften the dates in just-boiling water for 10 minutes. Drain and reserve ⅔ cup (160 ml) of the date soaking water. Blend the dates in a high-speed blender or mini food processor with ⅓ cup (80 ml) of the reserved water and the maple syrup. The dates will become a loose paste. If the paste is too thick, add additional reserved water 1 tablespoon (15 ml) at a time. Scrape the date mixture from the blender and add it to a small saucepan. You should have about ¾ to 1 cup (110 to 147 g).

When the cashews are done soaking, drain, rinse and blend them with ¾ cup (180 ml) of water in the blender. Set aside ⅓ cup (80 ml) of this cashew cream.

Caramelize the date mixture by cooking it in a small saucepan over medium heat while whisking continuously. After about 6 minutes it will begin to darken and become thicker. Be careful not to burn it.

Add the ⅓ cup (80 ml) of cashew cream, the butter, salt and vanilla extract. Continue to cook, while whisking, for 4 minutes. The mixture will begin to thicken and take on a caramel-like consistency. Remove the date caramel from the heat and carefully pour it into a small Mason jar. Store in the refrigerator.

RECIPE NOTES

Sure, apples dipped in caramel sauce are a go-to way to enjoy this sweet treat. But if you want to take this sauce to the next level, try using it as a topping on my 5-Ingredient French Toast (page 83).

Wondering what you should do with that extra cashew cream? Check out these recipes: Smashed Potatoes with French Onion Dip (page 98), Pasta Carbonara with Shiitake Mushroom "Bacon" (page 30) and Creamy Dill Dressing (page 146).

Cashew Butter Cup (N)ICE CREAM

SERVES
4

Vegan ice cream—also known as (n)ice cream—eluded me for a long time. Finding a suitable alternative to dairy cream proved to be a bit challenging. Then one day while I was making a batch of cashew cream sauce, it occurred to me to try using that as the base for my next batch of (n)ice cream. It worked. Beautifully. The second time. As it turns out, cashew cream has just a touch too much cashew flavor in it. My kids (and their friends) balked at it. So the next time I combined the cashew cream with oat milk. The result? A creamy, sweet answer to ice cream. For this version, I added chopped up bits of Justin's® Dark Chocolate Cashew Butter Cups. Dessert bliss.

1 cup (146 g) cashews

1¾ cups (420 ml) oat milk

½ cup (100 g) sugar

1 tsp salt

4 cashew butter cups (I like Justin's® Dark Chocolate Cashew Butter Cups), roughly chopped

Soak the cashews in 2 cups (480 ml) of just-boiling water. Set aside for 30 minutes.

Drain and rinse the cashews. In a high-speed blender, combine the cashews, oat milk, sugar and salt. Blend until creamy.

Add the mixture to your ice cream maker (see Recipe Notes). Churn for about 30 minutes, then add the chopped cashew butter cups. Continue to churn until frozen and creamy, about 15 minutes. This (n)ice cream will have a consistency similar to dairy ice cream. Serve immediately.

RECIPE NOTES

If you want to make this (n)ice cream in advance, you can freeze it in a freezer-safe container. You will need to remove it about 30 minutes before serving to allow it to soften.

No ice cream maker? That's okay! Just stir the cashew cup pieces into the blended mixture and pour it into a freezer-safe container. Allow to set for at least 4 hours. Remove 30 minutes before serving to soften.

MAKES
APPROXIMATELY
6 INDIVIDUAL
SERVINGS

It's a Cinch Chocolate **CHIA SEED PUDDING**

Ever scan the plant-based milk aisle at the market and wonder what on earth one does with all those different flavors? Me too. That is until I discovered chia seed pudding. Now that aisle is ripe with possibilities. One of my favorite recipes combines plant-based oat milk with chocolate and chia seeds to make an easy kid-friendly dessert.

½ cup (84 g) vegan semisweet chocolate chips (see Recipe Note)

1 tsp coconut oil

2 cups (480 ml) oak milk, slightly warmed

2 tbsp (30 ml) maple syrup

Pinch of salt

3 tbsp (30 g) chia seeds

Vegan dark chocolate slivers, for garnish (optional)

In a small microwave-safe bowl, combine the chocolate chips and coconut oil. Microwave on high in 30-second intervals until completely melted. Stir the chocolate in between sessions.

When the chocolate is fully melted, combine it with the oat milk, maple syrup and salt in a high-speed blender. Blend until smooth, then add the chia seeds and continue blending for a few more seconds.

Pour the mixture into individual serving dishes and refrigerate for at least 4 hours. Serve with dark chocolate slivers to garnish, if desired.

RECIPE NOTE

When looking for vegan chocolate, don't be deterred by the inclusion of "cocoa butter" on the ingredient list. Cocoa butter is the oil-based fat found in the cocoa bean and is a dairy-free ingredient.

Easy-As-Pie Peach GALETTE

SERVES
4

½ cup (114 g) + 1 tbsp
(14 g) cold vegan butter,
divided

¼ cup (31 g) all-purpose
flour

1 tsp salt

4 tbsp (60 ml) ice water

3 peaches (about 1½ lbs
[681 g]), divided

¼ cup (50 g) + 1 tbsp (15 g)
sugar, divided

1 tbsp (15 ml) fresh lemon
juice

2 tbsp (20 g) white chia
seeds

Remember how I talked about perfection in the introduction? This peach galette is the antithesis of perfection. Well, the shape of the crust is anyway. In terms of taste, it's out of this world. What I love about a galette is: (1) it's so easy to make, (2) it requires so few ingredients and (3) the crust is supposed to look rustic. The more you can make this look like it came out of the oven in a French farmhouse kitchen, the better.

Roughly cube the vegan butter and set aside in the refrigerator until ready to use.

To prepare the dough, combine the flour and salt in a food processor and pulse two to three times. Slowly add ½ cup (114 g) of the butter and pulse until well combined. The flour will take on a sandy composition. Add the ice water 1 tablespoon (15 ml) at a time while continuing to pulse. When a firm dough has formed, roll it into a ball, flatten it into a disc and wrap it in plastic wrap (or use an earth-friendly recycled plastic bread bag). Refrigerate for at least 30 minutes.

Slice one of the peaches into very thin wedges and set aside. These will serve as the topping. Roughly chop the other peaches. In a small saucepan, add the chopped peaches and ¼ cup (50 g) of sugar and simmer on low heat for 10 minutes. Then add the fresh lemon juice. The peaches will become syrupy and soft. As the peaches simmer, break them apart with a wooden spoon.

Preheat the oven to 400°F (205°C). Prepare a baking sheet with parchment paper or a silicone baking mat.

After the peaches have simmered, add the chia seeds to the saucepan. Stir to combine, then rest for 10 minutes. This will create a peach jam.

Roll out the dough into a thin, rough circle. Spread the peach jam onto the dough, leaving 1 to 1½ inches (2.5 to 4 cm) of space at the edges. Place the sliced peaches over the peach jam and gently fold the crust up over the jam, pleating the edges as you go.

Melt 1 tablespoon (14 g) of the butter and brush the edges of the crust with it. Sprinkle 1 tablespoon (15 g) of sugar over the peaches and the crust—I especially like sprinkled sugar on the crust!

Bake for 30 minutes on the middle rack. Remove the galette from the oven when the crust is golden brown and allow to cool for at least 20 minutes before serving.

SIMPLE SAUCES
and CONDIMENTS

This section holds many a key to good vegan cooking. Veganizing (my word) salads with Chipotle Ranch Dressing (page 145) and Creamy Dill Dressing (page 146) give them new flavor and life. You'll see my 15-Minute Strawberry Chia Seed Jam (page 133) and Easy Blueberry Compote (page 130) appear as healthier toppings to dishes like my 2-Step Overnight Oats (page 62) and 15-Minute Orange-Scented Waffles (page 76). None of those recipes require these additions, but I do like to offer these up as tasty options to round out my other vegan recipes.

MAKES
APPROXIMATELY
1 CUP (240 G)

Easy **BLUEBERRY COMPOTE**

It looks fancy, but this condiment is so simple! It uses just three non-staple ingredients, all of which are readily available at the grocery store. It's an excellent topping for my 15-Minute Orange-Scented Waffles (page 76). Honestly though, I'll smear it on saltine crackers when no one is looking. Or maybe eat it by the spoonful over the stove before anyone else in the family knows it exists.

2 cups (296 g) frozen blueberries, divided (see Recipe Note)

¼ cup (60 ml) maple syrup

1 tbsp (15 ml) fresh lemon juice

2 tbsp (20 g) chia seeds

In a small saucepan, combine 1 cup (148 g) of the frozen blueberries, 1 cup (240 ml) of water and the maple syrup. Bring to a simmer, stirring frequently, until the liquid is reduced to a thick syrup, about 10 minutes. Add the fresh lemon juice.

When thickened, add the remaining cup (148 g) of frozen blueberries. Cook until warmed through.

Remove the blueberry compote from the heat and stir in the chia seeds. As the compote cools, the chia seeds will absorb the liquid and it will thicken.

Once the compote has cooled, pour it into an airtight jar and store it in the refrigerator. Use the blueberry compote within 3 to 4 days.

RECIPE NOTE

I recommend using frozen blueberries for this recipe. The skin of the blueberry becomes softer after being frozen, making for a more desirable consistency when cooked.

15-Minute **STRAWBERRY CHIA SEED JAM**

Long gone are the days of sterilizing Mason jars and making jam with gelatin. Just kidding. I've never actually tried that. It just sounds so . . . dangerous. And why would I when you can make a simple fruit jam with just four ingredients? In this case, I chose strawberries as the main ingredient. The jam becomes thick with the inclusion of chia seeds—yet another vegan superfood. Chia seeds are rich in antioxidants, omega-3 and fiber—the latter of which makes them especially good at absorbing water.

2 cups (288 g) frozen strawberries

1 tsp fresh lemon juice

3 tbsp (30 g) chia seeds

1 tbsp (15 ml) maple syrup

Add the strawberries and 1 tablespoon (15 ml) of water to a small saucepan. Simmer on low heat, covered, for about 10 minutes, until the strawberries are soft. Using a wooden spoon, mash the strawberries to the desired size.

Add the lemon juice, chia seeds and maple syrup. Stir to combine.

When cool, pour the jam into a Mason jar and store in the refrigerator for 3 to 4 days.

MAKES
APPROXIMATELY
8 OUNCES (227 G)

5-Minute Vegan **"PARMESAN CHEESE"**

This condiment has a regular spot in my refrigerator. I use it to dress up any dish that I used to add Parmesan cheese to. It makes a great pizza topping. I also love sprinkling it on my Italian-inspired vegan dishes like Crispy Baked Eggplant with a Simple Homemade Tomato Sauce (page 41) or Penne alla Vodka (page 17). Creamy cashews and pine nuts give this seasoning a deep, rich flavor while the nutritional yeast, garlic and salt are a substitute for the pungency of Parmesan.

¼ cup (34 g) pine nuts (see Recipe Notes)

1 cup (146 g) roasted cashews (see Recipe Notes)

1 tsp salt

½ tsp onion powder

½ tsp garlic powder

1 tbsp (5 g) nutritional yeast

In a small, dry skillet set over medium heat, gently toast the pine nuts for 2 to 3 minutes until golden brown. The toasting will help add extra flavor to the "cheese."

Combine the toasted pine nuts, roasted cashews, salt, onion powder, garlic powder and nutritional yeast in a mini food processor. Blend until the nuts become fine pieces. Store in the refrigerator for up to a month.

RECIPE NOTES

Pine nuts are delicate and high in fat. This gives them a creamy consistency that adds richness to this dish. Because of the fat content they do burn quickly, so be sure to keep an eye on them as they're toasting.

Pre-roasted cashews can be purchased at the grocery store.

MAKES
APPROXIMATELY
12 OUNCES (340 G)

1 cup (143 g) blanched almonds

1 (5-oz [148-ml]) container almond milk yogurt

2 tbsp (10 g) nutritional yeast

1 tbsp (15 ml) lemon juice

½ tsp salt

Vegan "CREAM CHEESE"

For this recipe, I don't use cashews. Yes, I know. They're everywhere in my vegan cooking. It can't be helped. They offer up such a creamy texture. Here though, I wanted a slightly thicker texture and a milder flavor. So I opted for almonds. It's important to use blanched almonds (you can peel them yourself, but please, please, please buy them blanched. Save your mind and your fingers from unnecessary labor). Almond yogurt gives this "cream cheese" a slightly sour taste, just like the real thing.

Combine the almonds with 2 cups (480 ml) of water in a glass measuring cup. Cover and allow them to soak overnight.

Rinse and drain the soaked almonds. In a high-speed blender, combine the almonds, yogurt, nutritional yeast, lemon juice and salt. Blend until smooth and creamy. If the mixture is too thick, add water 1 tablespoon (15 ml) at a time.

Refrigerate in an airtight container for up to a week.

Simple Vegan **TERIYAKI SAUCE**

Who doesn't love teriyaki? This sticky-salty-sweet sauce is perhaps the perfect vegan comfort food. It's a great way to flavor tofu and give vegetables a little extra something. It's even good just drizzled over leftover rice. Not that you'd ever find me standing in front of an open fridge snacking on it. This recipe uses fresh garlic and ginger to give the sauce an enhanced spiciness, while the inclusion of rice wine vinegar gives it just the right amount of acidity.

1 tbsp (9 g) minced garlic
(see Recipe Notes)

1 tbsp (6 g) minced ginger
(see Recipe Notes)

½ cup (120 ml) tamari sauce

2 tbsp (30 ml) maple syrup

1 tbsp (15 ml) rice wine
vinegar

1 tbsp (8 g) cornstarch

In a small bowl, combine the garlic, ginger, tamari sauce, ½ cup (120 ml) of water, maple syrup and rice wine vinegar. Stir to combine.

In a separate bowl, mix 1 tablespoon (15 ml) of water with the cornstarch. Whisk to make a slurry. When smooth, add the mixture to the tamari marinade. Stir to combine.

Bring the sauce to a simmer in a small saucepan, stirring frequently. The cornstarch will cause the sauce to thicken as heat is applied, about 8 minutes. Allow to cool slightly. Store in a Mason jar in the refrigerator for up to 1 week.

RECIPE NOTES

Two large cloves of garlic are about equal to 1 tablespoon (9 g) of minced garlic.

A thumb-sized piece of fresh ginger is about equal to 1 tablespoon (6 g) of minced ginger.

MAKES
APPROXIMATELY
2 CUPS (216 G)

2-Step Homemade **BREADCRUMBS**

I maintain that homemade breadcrumbs (and croutons) should be used, always. They're so easy to make and using them in recipes like my Crispy Baked Eggplant with a Simple Homemade Tomato Sauce (page 41) and to top my Lemon-Garlic Pasta with Simple Spring Vegetables (page 21) takes these otherwise delightful recipes to a whole new level.

4 slices of bread (I like to use oat bread)

1 tsp salt

1 tbsp (3 g) Italian seasoning (see Recipe Note)

Toast the bread until well browned, but not burned.

Cut the bread into 1-inch (2.5-cm) pieces and combine with the salt and Italian seasoning in a mini food processor. Pulse until well combined. Refrigerate in an airtight container for up to 10 days.

RECIPE NOTE

You may think that using Italian seasoning is cheating, but I'm a big fan of herb and spice blends. Word on the street is that blends are often a way for herb and spice manufacturers to sell the dregs of their supply, so I do make an effort to shop high-quality brands. My favorite: Spice Jungle (www.spicejungle.com). The problem with a drawer full of individual spices is one of economy; they take up a lot of space, they can be costly and they don't last forever. The longer herbs and spices sit in your drawer, the less potent they become. It just makes sense to use blends.

MAKES
½ CUP (69 G)

Toasted **PUMPKIN SEEDS**

This simple 1-ingredient recipe (along with the tiniest touch of oil and a pinch of salt) makes a great topping for any number of dishes. Toasting the pumpkin seeds gives them some extra crunch and brings out their nutty flavor. I add pumpkin seeds (also known as pepitas) to my breakfast burritos, soups, salads . . . you name it and pumpkin seeds can probably complement it. Just check out their guest appearance on my Easy Jackfruit Taquitos (page 113)!

½ cup (69 g) pumpkin seeds

1 tsp safflower oil

½ tsp salt

Preheat the oven to 400°F (205°C). Toss the pumpkin seeds in the safflower oil.

Spread the pumpkin seeds out into a single layer on a baking sheet and bake for 6 minutes, stirring halfway through. You might hear popping as they toast. That is normal!

When the toasted seeds come out of the oven, sprinkle them with the salt and lay them out on a clean paper towel to cool. The paper towel will absorb any excess oil. Store them in an airtight container (I like a Mason jar) in a cool, dark place for up to 3 weeks.

MAKES
8 OUNCES
(240 ML)

Chipotle **RANCH DRESSING**

Ranch dressing with some attitude! The addition of a chipotle pepper with a touch of adobo sauce transforms this simple cashew cream ranch dressing into a seriously spicy condiment. I just love the combination of savory cream and kicky chipotle peppers! I use this dressing on my vegan taco salads, in my burritos and as a topping for dishes like my Easy Jackfruit Taquitos (page 113).

1 cup (146 g) cashews

1 clove garlic

2 tbsp (30 ml) fresh lemon juice

1 tsp salt

1 chipotle pepper in adobo sauce, roughly chopped

Soak the cashews in 2 cups (480 ml) of just-boiling water. Set aside for 30 minutes.

Drain and rinse the cashews. In a high-speed blender, combine the cashews and ¾ cup (180 ml) of water, the garlic, lemon juice, salt and chipotle pepper. Blend until creamy.

Store in the refrigerator for up to a week.

Creamy **DILL DRESSING**

Fresh dill is such a treat! I like to grow it in the summertime and use it to make things like dilly beans or this creamy dressing. This dressing pairs wonderfully with a simple side salad. It also works great as a dipping sauce for vegan appetizers, like my Less Mess Baked Breakfast Latkes (page 79).

1 cup (146 g) cashews

1 clove garlic

2 tbsp (30 ml) fresh lemon juice

1 tsp salt

1 tbsp (3 g) fresh dill + 1–2 sprigs for garnish, washed

1 tbsp (4 g) fresh parsley, washed and destemmed

Soak the cashews in 2 cups (480 ml) of just-boiling water. Set aside for 30 minutes.

Drain and rinse the cashews. In a high-speed blender, combine the cashews and ¾ cup (180 ml) of water, the garlic, lemon juice, salt, dill and parsley. Blend until creamy. Top with the reserved sprigs of dill.

Store in the refrigerator for up to a week.

Acknowledgments

There are many people to thank for helping me to write this book. As I've learned, encouragement to take on a project like this comes in a lot of different forms—all of them instrumental to getting the job done.

A very special thank-you to:

My husband, Greg, for enduring a perpetually messy kitchen; for trying the same recipe many times over; and for entertaining our kids so that I could write in peace.

My mom, Carol, and my mother-in-law, Myra, for their editing prowess. Without your help, this cookbook would have way too many commas.

My dad, JJ, and my father-in-law, Dan, for expressing their pride and managing my pre-pre-sales.

My beloved BHBs (my ski buddies, mountain bike mamas and all-around besties) for getting me out of my shell and supporting me always.

Jess, Kate, Danielle, Kristie, Kristen G., Kristen F., Jen G. and Ben for reading, rereading, rewriting and reviewing . . . and repeating.

Sara R. for enlightening me. There's no way I could have done this without you.

My publishing team at Page Street Publishing (Will, Madeline, Meg and Kylie) for your countless hours of work, your advice and insight and for taking a chance on me.

"Our Buddies"—my Instagram gang of fellow foodies—for being the best virtual cheerleaders a girl could ask for.

About the Author

Kate Friedman is the author behind the popular vegan blog Herbivore's Kitchen. A lifelong creative, Kate combined her love of cooking, writing, researching and photography with her desire to adopt a plant-based lifestyle into her online platform. In addition to sharing original vegan recipes, Kate enjoys profiling a variety of vegan-friendly ingredients and sharing insights into the life of a food blogger through her blog. When she's not in the kitchen, you can find Kate in the great outdoors hiking, biking, skiing or camping with her family.

Index